© Copyright 2024 - All rights reserved.

The content contained within this book may not be reproduced, duplicated or transmitted without direct written permission from the author or the publisher.

Under no circumstances will any blame or legal responsibility be held against the publisher, or author, for any damages, reparation, or monetary loss due to the information contained within this book, either directly or indirectly.

Legal Notice:

This book is copyright protected. It is only for personal use. You cannot amend, distribute, sell, use, quote or paraphrase any part, or the content within this book, without the consent of the author or publisher.

Disclaimer Notice:

Please note the information contained within this document is for educational and entertainment purposes only. All effort has been executed to present accurate, up to date, reliable, complete information. No warranties of any kind are declared or implied. Readers acknowledge that the author is not engaged in the rendering of legal, financial, medical or professional advice. The content within this book has been derived from various sources. Please consult a licensed professional before attempting any techniques outlined in this book.

By reading this document, the reader agrees that under no circumstances is the author responsible for any losses, direct or indirect, that are incurred as a result of the use of the information contained within this document, including, but not limited to, errors, omissions, or inaccuracies.

Table of Contents

INTRODUCTION 1

CHAPTER 1: LAYING THE FOUNDATION 5

HISTORY OF HEARTH AND HOME MAGIC 5
    Importance of Change 6
    Spell for Inviting Change: Your Front Door 6
    Psychology of Home 8
DEFINING WHAT "SPIRITUAL" MEANS TO YOU 11
    What Does It Mean to Be Sacred? 11
    Protecting and Respecting the Home 12
THE SACRED HEARTH 12
    Preparing Your Home for Major Life Changes or Transitions 13
COPING WITH CHALLENGES 13
    Cleaning and Renewing Your Space as You Progress 14
    Overcoming Fear or Anxiety About Your Craft 14

CHAPTER 2: CREATING A MAGICAL HOME 17

LOOK FOR BEAUTY AS ENERGY IN YOUR HOME 17
    Beauty Within the Four Basic Elements—Fire, Earth, Air, and Water 18
    Magical Materials: Building Blocks to Beauty 19
    Color Magic at Home 19
    Natural Textures Like Wood, Wool, Stone, Water, Fungi, and Crystals 20
    Herbs and Oils 21
ROOM-BY-ROOM DECLUTTERING AND CLEANING 21
    Bedroom Magic 23
    Bathroom and Cleaning 23
    Sitting Rooms and Social Spaces 24
    Landings and Passageways 24
LIGHT AND ITS USES 25
    Include and Delight in the Magic of Modernity 26

CHAPTER 3: TENDING THE HEARTH 31

CONNECTION TO THE MAGIC OF NATURE AND HIGHER SELF 31
    Cultural Traditions and Behaviors 32
    Sacred Spaces 33
    The Sacred Hearth 35
THE CAULDRON: HISTORY, IMPORTANCE, AND SYMBOLISM TODAY 37

Harnessing the Element of Fire Magic Safely 37
Candle Magic at Home—Spells by Light 38
Incense and Oils—Domestic Ritual 39
Warmth, Comfort, and Protection Spells 41
Eating by Candlelight 41
Nurturing Relationships With Hearth Magic 42
Welcoming Guests With Warmth and Blessings 42
Creating a Peaceful Environment for Disagreements 43
Home Magic for Love and Friendship 44

CHAPTER 4: RECIPES, SPELLS, AND RITUALS TO CREATE A MAGICAL HOME 47

LIST OF ELEMENTS AND MATERIALS FOR CASTING SPELLS AND PERFORMING RITUALS 47
    Elements 47
    Materials for Spells and Rituals 49
SPIRITUAL PRACTICES: LISTENING TO THE VOICE OF YOUR HOME 51
    Asking for Guidance Ritual 51
    Looking Inward Ritual 52
    Listening to the Voice of Our Home 53
    Morning Ritual 54
    Enchanting Ritual for the Evening 55
PRACTICAL RITUALS FOR CLEANING AND SPIRITUAL PURIFICATION 56
    Cleaning Ritual 56
    Smudging Ritual 57
    Spiritual Purification of Each Room 58
RITUALS TO RECOGNIZE THE SANCTITY OF EACH SPACE 60
    Bedroom Sanctification Ritual 60
    Grounding and Meditative Practices 61
    Practical Rituals for Cleansing 62
    Recognizing and Honoring Each Space—Kitchen Blessing 62
ENERGY MAINTENANCE 63

CHAPTER 5: MAGIC OF THE HEARTH AND KITCHEN 67

THE POWER AND HISTORY OF THE KITCHEN SPACE 67
    Setting up Your Kitchen With Spirit 68
    Kitchen History and How It Has Evolved to Today 68
    Your Feelings About Kitchen Work 69
    Renewing Our Magical Kitchen Practices 70
KITCHEN SHRINES AND ALTARS 71
USING THE ELEMENTS TO CREATE SPELLS AND SPIRITUAL FOODS 72
    An Example of Elemental Cooking Meditation 73
    Slow Down: The Magic Is in the Detail 73

CHAPTER 6: KITCHENCRAFT AND THE GIFT OF FOOD 77

KITCHENCRAFT AND THE SPIRITUALITY AND GIFT OF FOOD 77

- *The Spirit of Generosity* 78
- FORAGING BASICS 79
  - *Unprocessed Food and Thinking* 80
- ORIGINS AND SIGNIFICANCE OF INGREDIENTS 81
  - *Ingredients Place in Your Life* 82
- COOKING MINDFULLY AND SLOWLY 83
- THE IMPORTANCE OF EMOTIONAL STATE IN COOKING 84
  - *The Power of Positive Energy in Food* 85
  - *Creating a Sacred Dining Space* 86
  - *Cooking Spell to Bless Your Abundance in the Kitchen* 86

CHAPTER 7: MAGICAL FOOD RECIPES FOR SPIRITUAL AND PHYSICAL NOURISHMENT AND HEALTH 89

- SEASONALITY AND ITS USE 89
  - *Harnessing Seasonal Energy in Your Cooking* 90
- THE MAGIC OF BREADMAKING 91
  - *Simple Herb-Infused Bread (Tiffany, 2022)* 92
- THE HISTORY OF STEWS AND BROTHS 94
  - *Magical Hearty Harvest Stew (Megan, 2021)* 94
  - *Healing Herbal Broth (Natasha, 2020)* 96
- THE HISTORY OF ROASTS 98
  - *Magical Herb-Encrusted Roast Beef (Herb-Crusted Roast Beef, 2023)* 98
- THE HISTORY OF VEGETABLES IN COOKING 100
  - *Magical Roasted Root Vegetables (Elkus, 2023)* 100
- THE HISTORY OF FUNGI IN COOKING 102
  - *Magical Creamy Mushroom Soup (Karina, 2018)* 102
- HERBS FOR COOKING 104

CHAPTER 8: MAINTAINING THE BALANCE OF HEARTH AND HOME 107

- GET TO KNOW YOUR CORNER OF THE UNIVERSE 107
  - *Wheel of Seasons, Weathers, Stars, and Moon Energy* 108
- PURPOSEFUL SEASONAL RITUALS AND ACTIONS 111
  - *Planting Seeds of Intention: A Spring Ritual* 111
  - *Celebrating Abundance and Vitality in the Summer: A Ritual* 112
  - *Harvesting and Reflection: An Autumn Ritual* 113
  - *Resting and Releasing: A Winter Ritual* 114
- MAINTAINING BALANCE THROUGH THE SEASONS 115
  - *Wheel of the Year Celebrations at Home* 116
  - *Elemental Balancing Through the Seasons* 119
  - *Elemental Balancing Meditation* 120

CHAPTER 9: FUTURE OF HEARTH MAGIC AND THE ROLE OF MODERN WITCH 123

- WHO AND WHERE ARE THE MODERN WITCHES? 123
- PURPOSE AND POWER IN CONNECTING WITH WITCHCRAFT 124

    Innovation in Modern Witchcraft: New Trends and Techniques *125*
    Digital Moon Ritual *128*
TECHNO-WITCHERY: INCLUDING DIGITAL TOOLS IN YOUR PRACTICE 129
SUSTAINABLE WITCHCRAFT PRACTICES FOR EARTH-FRIENDLY CHOICES..........................130
    Sustainable Full Moon Ritual..*131*
DIGITAL WITCHERY OF TODAY 133
    New Ways to Travel and Connect to the Universal Song of Wicca.............*134*
    Creating a Virtual Altar for Digital Witchery *135*
SUCCESSION PLANNING: PASSING ON YOUR HEARTH WISDOM 136
    Harnessing Hearth Magic Beyond Physical Presence *137*

CONCLUSION.. 139

GLOSSARY 141

REFERENCES 147

Introduction

Your sacred space is where you can find yourself again and again. –Joseph Campbell

Amid the rush of our busy, often complex lives and the hum of modern technology, a quiet mystical revolution is unfolding. Our instincts speak to us at times of change in our lives, and they remind us that we each hold a vast amount of inner wisdom and knowledge. You already know about your instincts; perhaps they brought you to this book today. You will know the power of connecting with your inner voice, the natural world, and your ability to transform your surroundings into a sanctuary of beauty, balance, and magic. This is the realm of the modern witch—a blend of ancient wisdom and contemporary insights—where our inner and outer lives dance in harmony.

But who is the modern witch? They could be anyone: your neighbor, colleague, or the person next to you in a cafe, using a sprig of rosemary, or whispering intentions over her tea. Modern witches come from all walks of life and are united by a shared commitment to living with intention and deeply connecting with the natural world. They weave magic and ritual into the fabric of their everyday existence and transform the mundane into the mystical with each thoughtful act.

This book is for you, dear reader, whether you are starting over, seeking a deeper connection with your home, or embarking on a journey of self-discovery. It's for those who wish to reinvent their lives and spaces using modern witchcraft wisdom, beauty, and power. By weaving rituals and ancient practices into the fabric of your everyday life, you can transform your home into a magical haven that nurtures your body, mind, and spirit.

The origins of witchcraft are as ancient as humanity itself and are part of the history of every culture and civilization. From the wise women and seers of old, revered for their knowledge of healing herbs and their ability to be immune to and embrace the unseen, to the empiric healers of medieval Europe, who practiced in secret to avoid persecution, the essence of witchcraft has always been about harnessing natural energies for healing, protection, and transformation.

Modern witches are reclaiming this heritage, bringing it into the light of the 21st century. Hearth and kitchen magic are central to this reclamation. In ancient times, the hearth was the heart of the home, where food was prepared and families gathered. This tradition continues as modern witches infuse their daily routines with intention and magic. Stirring a pot of soup with a clockwise motion to invite prosperity or placing a sprig of rosemary by the door for protection are simple yet powerful ways to integrate magic ritual into everyday life.

I, Aphra Devereux, am a modern witch, artist, interior designer, and maker. My journey on this path began in the heart of the English countryside. Raised in a lineage of powerful matriarchs, I spent my formative years surrounded by the warmth and wisdom of my grandmother, mother, and aunts. We spent many hours in the family kitchens, places of power and secret knowledge. Here, I unknowingly absorbed the ancient craft passed down through generations, learning the sacred rhythms of life's cycles and the art of restarting. This last tool I now seamlessly integrate into my work as an interior designer, intuitively guiding clients through the spatial transformations of their homes and places of beauty and sanctity.

Drawing from the rich tapestry of pagan and witchcraft philosophy, I bring a deep understanding of natural rhythms and harmonious living to my practice. For me, witchcraft is a belief system and a practical and logical approach to navigating the complexities of human existence. Through my love for the power of home and the transformative potential of rituals, I have woven together the threads of ancient wisdom and modern design to create spaces that resonate with intention and magic.

I take my place as a link in the chain of thousands of magical practices, honoring the diverse cultural interpretations and traditions that have shaped my craft. In times of challenge and change, I turn to the solid and trustworthy sources of witchcraft for guidance and resilience, drawing strength from the timeless wisdom that has sustained generations before me. Through my work and life, I continue exploring the boundless possibilities of witchcraft, seeking to inspire others to awaken the magic within and around them.

In this book, you will uncover how modern witchcraft can enrich your life. From reclaiming the sacred sanctity of home to using color magic for energy, mood, and focus, you will learn practical ways to integrate witchcraft into your daily routine. The book is roughly divided into three sections, each addressing a fundamental human need:

- **Shelter:** Learn how to create a sacred, harmonious space that reflects your values and supports your spiritual journey.

- **Food:** Discover the art of kitchen witchery, where cooking and food preparation become magic and nourishment for the soul.

- **A place to belong:** Establish a powerful foundation to engage with the world, fostering a sense of belonging and purpose.

By embracing the principles and power of magic, you will develop a new relationship with your home, body, and outlook on life. My wish for you is to be open to ancient information in the following pages. Use this magical guide to start transforming your home and hearth, using modern witchcraft's wisdom, beauty, and power to create your sacred spiritual sanctuary. Enjoy!

Chapter 1:

Laying the Foundation

There is a voice that doesn't use words. Listen. –Rumi

Learning how to use witchcraft in our everyday lives is a sacred journey. Know that every step is a dance of intention and transformation. We are reminded that change is inevitable and essential—it is a catalyst for growth, magic, and personal evolution. This chapter will lay the foundation for our journey and prepare the fertile ground for new beginnings and ancient wisdom to take root.

History of Hearth and Home Magic

There is a reason why witches' homes are alive in all of the stories! Witches know all households are home not only to humans and pets but also to spirits and deities that protect the house and care for all the inhabitants. Your house senses you and knows who you are. Make sure to talk to your house! Your house is a sentient being with its own consciousness. When you enter your house, greet all those who live there, and when you leave, say thank you. Your home will acknowledge your attention.

Across all times, cultures, and epochs, the hearth has symbolized the heart of the home. Your fireside is a place of warmth, nourishment, and spiritual connection. In ancient Rome, the goddess Vesta was worshiped as the guardian of the hearth, her eternal flame representing the soul of the home and the continuity of life. Similarly, in Norse tradition, the hearth was sacred to Friigg, the goddess of home and motherhood, who blessed households with love and protection.

In Celtic cultures, the hearth was a sacred space for kitchen witchery, where wise women brewed potions and crafted charms to heal and protect their families.

Importance of Change

Change is the heartbeat of life—a constant pulse that propels us forward on our journey. Whether they are beginnings or endings, life transitions hold the potential for profound transformation. Just as the seasons shift and the moon waxes and wanes, our lives are marked by cycles of growth and renewal. As I mentioned, I learned as a child that there is a very useful life skill that we can hone: the art of restarting. Embrace this!

Preparing for change involves setting intentions, releasing what no longer serves us, and welcoming new possibilities with an open heart. By working with the natural rhythms of life, we align ourselves with the flow of the universe, making space for new magic and opportunities to enter our lives.

Spell for Inviting Change: Your Front Door

The entrance to your home is more than just a passageway—it is a powerful portal that can influence energy flow into your living space. By consciously working with your front door, you can create an inviting threshold that welcomes positive opportunities and transformative experiences. In the following spells, we will harness the magical properties of salt, cinnamon, and rosemary to protect and attract good fortune.

Enticing Opportunities and Inviting Change

This spell uses salt, cinnamon, and rosemary, ingredients known for their properties of good fortune and protection.

Materials needed

- salt
- ground cinnamon
- a sprig of fresh rosemary
- a small dish or bowl

Steps

1. Clean the area around your front door, ensuring it is free from clutter and dirt. A clean and welcoming entryway is essential for inviting positive energy into your home.

2. In a small dish, combine the salt and ground cinnamon. As you mix, focus your intention on inviting good fortune and positive change into your home. Visualize these energies blending in the mixture.

3. Speaking intentionally into spaces changes the energy of that space. This is called 'casting a spell', or 'throwing the spell' into the space. Take a pinch of the salt and cinnamon mixture and sprinkle it across the threshold of your front door. As you do, say aloud: "Salt and cinnamon, blend and bind. Good fortune and change will be mine to find. Protect this space, let opportunities come, and by this threshold, welcome all to come."

4. Take the sprig of rosemary and place it above your front door. If you cannot place it directly above the door, you can hang it nearby or in a small pot close to the entryway. As you place the rosemary, say, "Rosemary, guardian at the door, protect this home always. Keep out harm, and let blessings flow. Welcome change and make it so."

5. Stand at your front door and take a moment to visualize your home as a beacon of positive change and good fortune. Feel the protective and inviting energy settling around your

entrance. Conclude the spell by saying, "By salt, by spice, by herb divine, this home is blessed: opportunities align. So will it be."

Psychology of Home

Our homes are physical structures—sanctuaries that hold our memories, emotions, and energy. The psychology of home explores our deep emotional connections to our living spaces and how they reflect our inner world. A well-loved home can be a source of comfort, stability, and inspiration, while a neglected or chaotic space can contribute to feelings of stress and unease (Roster et al., 2016).

Research has shown that the environment we create around us significantly impacts our mental and emotional well-being. A study published in the Journal of Environmental Psychology found that people who described their homes as restive and restorative experienced lower levels of psychological distress (Chowdhury, 2019). By consciously designing our living spaces to support our emotional needs, we can cultivate peace, creativity, and healing.

Finding Your Inner Sanctuary and Tools for Self-Discovery

Creating a sacred space within our homes is a powerful tool for self-discovery and spiritual growth. Our inner sanctuary becomes a place where we can retreat from the outside world, reconnect with our inner selves, and practice our craft in peace and solitude. Finding your inner sanctuary begins with identifying a space in your home that feels intuitively right for you—maybe it's a cozy corner, a dedicated room, or even an outdoor garden.

Once you have found your space, fill it with items that resonate with your spirit and intentions. This might include crystals, candles, herbs, sacred symbols, and personal mementos. Each object should hold meaning and purpose, contributing to the overall energy of the space. Work on getting rid of anything that does not lift your heart. Be ruthless. As you spend time in your sanctuary, you will find that it becomes a powerful anchor for your spiritual practice—a place where you can meditate, reflect, and cast your spells.

In addition to creating a physical sanctuary, it's important to cultivate tools for self-discovery. Journaling, meditation, and tarot reading are powerful practices that can help you explore your inner landscape and gain insight into your path. A modern witch knows that our inner voice is our spiritual guide and is our connection to our truth.

Begin by walking slowly through your home. Pause in each room and reflect on how you occupy the space. What do you do in each room? Where do you spend most of your time? For instance, you might sit in a specific corner to read, work at a particular table, or rush through a hallway on your way out.

Now, try doing things differently. Sit on different chairs or sleep in another room. You may discover that other spaces reveal new insights and sensations. Feel each place and current activity—how light falls, colors and textures, and favorite objects. Consider removing or packing away all that you don't love.

To aid in this journey of discovery and transformation, let's perform a simple spell to connect more deeply with your home and inner sanctuary.

A Spell to Connecting to Your Inner Sanctuary

You will need

- a white candle (for clarity and purification)
- a small bowl of water (representing emotion and intuition)
- a handful of salt (for grounding and protection)
- a sprig of fresh rosemary or sage (for wisdom and clarity)

Steps

1. **Prepare your space.** Find a quiet room where you can perform this spell undisturbed and be comfortable. Light the white candle and place it in front of you. Position the bowl of water and the salt nearby. Hold the rosemary or sage in your hands.

2. **Set your intention.** Close your eyes and take three deep breaths, grounding yourself in the present moment. Visualize a white light surrounding you, offering protection and clarity. Set the intention to connect deeply with your home and your inner sanctuary.

3. **Bless the water.** Hold the bowl of water in your hands and say: "Water of life, flow within me. Reveal the truths I need to see." Sprinkle a pinch of salt into the water, stirring it with your finger.

4. **Cleanse with rosemary or sage.** Take the sprig of rosemary or sage and gently wave it through the air, allowing its fragrance to cleanse the space around you. As you do this, say: "Herb of wisdom, herb of light, clear my mind, enhance my sight."

5. **Walk through your home.** Slowly walk through each room with the bowl of blessed water and the rosemary or sage. Pause in each room, dip your fingers into the water, and flick a few drops around the space. Say: "By water and earth, air and fire, reveal my inspiring spaces. Show me where I feel most free, guide my heart, so let it be."

6. **Reflect and reassess.** Return to your starting point and sit quietly. Reflect on what you felt and observed in each room. Which spaces resonated with you? Where did you feel discomfort or stagnation?

7. **Express gratitude.** Blow out the candle, giving thanks for the clarity and guidance received. Take a moment to express gratitude for your home and the sanctuary it provides.

Defining What "Spiritual" Means to You

Embarking on the path of modern witchcraft requires a personal understanding of what "spiritual" means to you. For some, spirituality is an intimate and unique journey, a connection to something greater that involves a relationship with the divine or nature. For others, it could be about connecting with the inner self, the universe, or ancestral wisdom.

To help define your spirituality, consider what resonates with your soul. Is it the feeling of peace you get when walking in nature, the quiet moments of meditation, the ritual that honors the cycles of the moon, or the joy of creating a nurturing life through herbalism and kitchen magic? Spirituality is about finding what makes your heart sing, what brings you peace, and what helps you navigate the complexities of life with grace and intention.

What Does It Mean to Be Sacred?

To be sacred means to be connected to something greater, to hold space, or to perform an act in reverence and respect. The sacredness of home is about recognizing and honoring your living space as a sanctuary, a place of refuge and spiritual nourishment. It is about infusing your home with intention, creating an environment that supports and enhances your well-being and spiritual practice.

To create sacredness in your home, you must consider both physical and energetic aspects. Physically, this means keeping your home clean, organized, and filled with items that bring joy and peace. Energetically, this involves practices such as smudging, using crystals, and setting intentions to clear and uplift the energy of your space. By treating your home as a sacred space, you honor it as a vital part of your spiritual journey, where you can retreat, rejuvenate, and connect with your higher self.

Protecting and Respecting the Home

Protecting and respecting the home is a fundamental aspect of hearthcraft. Just as you would guard your physical and emotional well-being, safeguarding your home ensures that it remains a place of safety and tranquility. This involves practical measures and magical practices to maintain a harmonious and secure environment.

On a practical level, protecting your home can mean securing doors and windows, creating a clean and clutter-free space, and ensuring your living environment is safe and healthy. On a magical level, it involves setting up protective wards, using symbols and talismans, and performing regular energy cleansing.

One simple, powerful way to protect your home is by creating a protective boundary using salt, crystals, or herbs such as rosemary and lavender. You can also invoke protective deities or spirits, asking them to watch over your home and keep it safe from harm. Respecting the home means recognizing its role as a sanctuary, being mindful of the energy you bring into your space, showing gratitude for its shelter and comfort, and maintaining a harmonious environment through regular rituals and offerings.

The Sacred Hearth

The hearth has long been the heart of the home. It is a central and sacred space that represents warmth, nourishment, and communal life. It is where families gather, meals are prepared, and stories are told, creating a sense of continuity and connection.

Spiritually, the hearth fire represents the fire of life, creation, and transformation. In many traditions, it is seen as a conduit for prayers and intentions, carrying them to the divine. Tending the hearth fire can involve rituals such as lighting candles with specific intentions, using fire-safe herbs for cleansing and protection, and maintaining a clean and orderly hearth area as a sign of respect for sacred spaces.

Your spiritual hearth is the central part of your home where you feel the most connected to your inner self and the energies around you. It might be a literal hearth, a kitchen, or any other space that feels sacred and nurturing. Finding your spiritual hearth involves tuning into your intuition and sensing where you feel the most grounded and at peace in your home.

Once you have located your spiritual hearth, you can access its energy by spending time there, meditating, and performing rituals. Create an altar or a dedicated space to honor them, using photos, heirlooms, or offerings that resonate with your heritage and lineage. This practice acknowledges the wisdom and support of those who came before you, integrating their presence into your daily life.

Preparing Your Home for Major Life Changes or Transitions

Major life changes and transitions, such as moving to a new home, starting a new job, or experiencing significant personal growth, require physical and energetic preparation. Preparing your home for these changes involves creating a supportive environment that adapts and responds to new energies and circumstances.

Start by decluttering and cleaning your home, removing items that no longer serve you, and making space for new beginnings. This physical act of clearing can also help to release stagnant energy and create a sense of openness and possibility. Next, consider performing a space-clearing ritual to purify and uplift your home's energy. This can involve smudging with sage or other cleansing herbs, using sound (such as bells or singing bowls), and setting intentions for the new phase of your life.

Coping With Challenges

Challenges are inevitable when you begin exploring the world of the modern witch and hearth craft. These challenges might come from self-doubt, external obstacles, or unexpected changes. Coping with these challenges requires resilience, adaptability, and a deep trust in your power and the transformation process.

A way to overcome these doubts is to establish meaningful daily rituals that ground and connect you to your intentions. This might include meditation, journaling, or performing small rituals that reinforce your sense of purpose and direction. Additionally, surrounding yourself with a supportive community, whether it is fellow practitioners, friends, or family, can provide encouragement and perspective during difficult times.

Another powerful tool for coping with challenges is using affirmations and positive self-talk. Remind yourself of your strengths, progress, and capacity to overcome obstacles.

Cleaning and Renewing Your Space as You Progress

As you grow and evolve in your practice, it's essential to regularly cleanse and renew your space to keep the energy vibrant and aligned with your intentions. Cleaning your space can involve both physical cleaning and energetic clearing.

Physically, this means continuing to keep your home tidy and free of clutter, which helps to maintain a sense of order and clarity. Energetically, you can cleanse your space using smudging, sound, or salt. Smudging with herbs like sage, palo santo, or rosemary can help to clear away negative energy and invite positive vibrations. Soul cleansing, using bells, chimes, or singing bowls, can also help shift the energy of a space. Sprinkling salt around the perimeter of your home or using it in a floor wash can further purify and protect your space.

Overcoming Fear or Anxiety About Your Craft

It's common to experience fear or anxiety about your craft, especially if you are new to witchcraft or when social stigmas and misconceptions have influenced your perception. Overcoming these fears requires education, self-compassion, and practice. There is much for you to discover! Go gently. Your instincts will guide you.

Continue to educate yourself about witchcraft, its history, and its practices. Understanding the craft's roots and diversity can demystify it and help you feel more confident in your path. Find reputable sources, connect with experienced practioners, and engage in community discussions to build your knowledge and support network.

Practicing self-compassion is also crucial. Recognize that fear and anxiety are natural responses to the unknown and permit yourself to feel these emotions without judgment. Explore grounding techniques, such as deep breathing, meditation, or spending time in nature, to center yourself and reduce anxiety.

Dealing With Negative Energies and Spirits

Negative energies and spirits can sometimes intrude into our lives and spaces, disrupting the harmony and peace we strive to maintain. Dealing with these entities requires a combination of protective measures, cleansing rituals, and assertive intention-setting.

Protective measures include setting wards around your home, using protective crystals like black tourmaline or obsidian, and creating protective charms or sigils (magic symbols). Regularly cleansing your space, as mentioned earlier, can help to keep negative energies at bay.

If you encounter a negative spirit, staying calm and assertive is important. Politely but firmly ask the spirit to leave, stating that your space is protected and only positive, loving energies are welcome. You can use tools such as licensed holy water or protective prayers to reinforce your intent. If you feel overwhelmed, don't hesitate to seek assistance from a more experienced practitioner or a spiritual advisor.

Healing as a Way Forward

Healing is a central practice of witchcraft, serving as both a goal and a method. Whether you are healing from physical ailments, emotional wounds, or spiritual disconnections, the healing process is integral to moving forward and achieving personal transformation.

Herbalism plays a significant role in healing. Using herbs and plants for their medicinal properties can aid in physical recovery and emotional balance. Lavender for stress, chamomile for relaxation, and eucalyptus for respiratory issues are just a few examples of how nature provides remedies for our well-being.

Emotional and spiritual healing often involves deeper introspection and intentional practices. Techniques such as shadow work, where you confront and integrate the darker aspects of yourself, can be profoundly transformative. Journaling, guided meditations, and therapy can also support emotional healing by providing clarity and releasing suppressed feelings.

In this chapter, we've explored coping with challenges, cleansing and renewing our spaces, overcoming fears, dealing with negative energies, and the profound journey of healing. As we lay this foundation, we prepare ourselves for the transformative path ahead, equipped with the knowledge, tools, and spirit to embrace the magic of hearth craft and personal transformation.

Chapter 2:

Creating a Magical Home

Clear space. Make room for what's coming. —Nakeia Homer

In this chapter, we embark on transforming your living space into a sanctuary of serenity and spiritual rejuvenation and we'll explore the art of creating a magical home. In this place, you can nurture your soul, find inner peace, and reconnect with your spiritual essence. From decluttering and cleansing rituals to the strategic integration of interior design elements, such as color, texture, and sacred spaces, we'll delve into the power your environment has on your spiritual well-being. Prepare to take a transformative journey as we unlock the secrets to crafting a home that reflects your innermost desires and nurtures your spiritual growth and vitality.

Look for Beauty as Energy in Your Home

Cultivating positive and balanced energy within your home is essential for nurturing your spiritual well-being. Begin by creating spaces of beauty that make your heart sing and evoke feelings of peace, joy, and serenity.

This entails decluttering and organizing your surroundings, allowing chi (life force energy) to flow freely throughout your home. Integrate elements of nature, such as plants, crystals, and natural materials, to ground and uplift the energy of your space.

Take a moment to pause and look with fresh eyes at your home, seeing beyond the surface to the essence of its soul. Notice the little detail that brings you joy—a sunlit window seat, a cherished heirloom passed down through generations, or the comforting embrace of a cozy blanket. Amplify these elements of beauty and love, infusing your home with warmth, personality, and authenticity. Surround yourself with objects and decor that resonate with your soul, creating a space that reflects your unique journey and aspirations.

Beauty Within the Four Basic Elements—Fire, Earth, Air, and Water

Embrace the elemental forces of fire, earth, air, and water, weaving them seamlessly into the fabric of your magical home. Each element holds its own unique energy and symbolism, contributing to your space's overall harmony and balance.

- **Fire:** Symbolizing passion, vitality, and transformation, fire infuses your home with warmth and energy. Incorporate candles, lanterns, or a fireplace to evoke the flickering flames of inspiration and creativity.

- **Earth:** Grounding and nurturing, earth energy provides stability and security within your home. Invite the grounding presence of earth into your space with natural materials such as wood, stone, and clay. Decorate with plants and crystals to connect with the earth's healing energies and foster a sense of abundance and growth.

- **Air:** Representing intellect, communication, and clarity, air energy brings a fresh perspective into your home. Keep your space well-ventilated and clutter-free to allow the air to circulate freely. Include elements of air, such as feathers, wind chimes, or aromatic diffusers, to promote mental clarity, inspiration, and open communication.

- **Water:** Flowing and adaptable, water energy encourages emotional healing, intuition, and fluidity. Integrate the soothing presence of water into your home with fountains, bowls of water, or artwork depicting serene aquatic scenes. Allow the gentle sound of flowing water to calm your mind, cleanse your spirit, and invite emotional balance and renewal.

Magical Materials: Building Blocks to Beauty

Materials play a crucial role in the energy and ambiance of your home. By thoughtfully selecting colors, textures, and natural elements, you can create a space that signifies your spirit and enhances your well-being.

Color Magic at Home

By consciously choosing colors that align with your intentions, you can create spaces that support your physical, emotional, and spiritual well-being.

- **Energy boost:** Include vibrant colors like red, orange, and yellow in areas where you need an energy boost, such as the kitchen or workout space.

- **Mood enhancement:** Use calming colors like blue, green, and soft neutrals in bedrooms and living areas to enhance relaxation and emotional well-being.

- **Focus and clarity:** Create productive workspaces with colors that stimulate mental clarity and focus, such as shades of green and blue.

Color is a powerful tool in home magic; each hue carries unique vibrations and symbolism. Understanding the magical properties of colors allows you to employ their energies to influence the mood and atmosphere of your space.

- **Red:** A vibrant and intense color, red symbolizes passion, energy, and strength. Use red accents to invigorate a space and ignite a sense of motivation and action.

- **Blue:** Representing calm, peace, and tranquility, blue is perfect for creating serene and soothing environments. Include shades of blue in areas where relaxation and reflection are desired.

- **Green:** The color of growth, balance, and renewal; green brings the energy of nature into your home. Use green to promote healing and harmony, especially in living areas and bedrooms.

- **Yellow:** Bright and cheerful; yellow symbolizes happiness, creativity, and clarity. Add yellow elements to spaces where you need to boost your mood and inspire creativity.

- **Purple:** Associated with spirituality, wisdom, and intuition, purple is ideal for meditation spaces or areas where you seek deeper insight and connection.

Natural Textures Like Wood, Wool, Stone, Water, Fungi, and Crystals

Natural materials bring the essence of the earth into your home, grounding and harmonizing the energy within your space.

- **Woods:** Wood embodies strength, stability, and growth. Include wooden furniture, flooring, or decor to create a warm and nurturing environment.

- **Wool:** Soft and comforting; wool symbolizes warmth and protection. Use woolen textiles like blankets, rugs, and cushions to add coziness and comfort.

- **Stone:** Stone and minerals are grounding elements that connect us to the earth's core energy. Decorate with stone accents or crystals to foster stability and balance.

- **Water:** The presence of water elements, such as fountains or aquariums, brings fluidity, cleansing, and tranquility to your home.

- **Fungi:** Mushrooms and fungi represent transformation and the interconnectedness of life. Include decorative fungi motifs or actual fungi terrariums to remind you of nature's magic.

- **Crystals:** Crystals hold unique vibrational properties that can enhance your home's energy. Use crystals like amethyst for spiritual growth, rose quartz for love, and clear quartz for clarity and amplification of intentions.

Herbs and Oils

Herbs and oils are potent allies in creating a magical home, bringing the essence of nature into your living space. They can be used for cleansing, protecting, and enhancing your environment's overall energy.

- **Sage:** Known for its purifying properties, sage is used in smudging rituals to cleanse and clear negative energy.

- **Lavender:** With its calming and soothing aroma, lavender promotes relaxation and peace. Use lavender sachets, essential oils, or fresh sprigs to infuse your home tranquility.

- **Rosemary:** Symbolizing protection and clarity, rosemary can be used in cooking, dried bundles, and essential oils to purify the air and mind.

- **Cinnamon:** This warming spice brings abundance, prosperity, and protection. Use cinnamon sticks or essential oils to enhance your home's energy.

- **Eucalyptus:** Known for its refreshing and invigorating scent, eucalyptus clears the air and promotes healing. Use eucalyptus leaves in showers or diffusers for a revitalizing effect.

Room-By-Room Decluttering and Cleaning

Transforming your home into a magical haven requires a thoughtful approach to each room, ensuring that every space is harmonious, balanced, and infused with positive energy. Let's explore how to rejuvenate your home room by room, using principles from Feng Shui. This ancient Chinese practice of harmonizing your environment is crucial in creating a balanced and energetically vibrant home. By arranging your living spaces according to Feng Shui principles, you can enhance the flow of chi (life force energy) and promote health, happiness, and prosperity.

- **Declutter, re-order, and rebalance:** Start by decluttering each room, removing items that no longer serve you or bring joy. A clutter-free space allows energy to flow freely, reducing stress and promoting clarity. Re-order your belongings in a balanced and harmonious way, ensuring each item has a designated place.

- **Cleanse:** Cleaning your home energetically is as important as physical cleaning. Use sage smudging, palo santo, or essential oil diffusers to clear stagnant energy and invite fresh, positive vibrations. Regularly cleanse your space to maintain a high energetic frequency.

- **Add color and comfort:** Introduce colors that align with the intended energy of each room. Use soft, calming hues in bedrooms, vibrant colors in social spaces, and soothing tones in bathrooms. Enhance comfort with cozy textiles, plush pillows, and inviting furniture arrangements.

- **Infuse magic:** Infuse each room with elements of magic, whether through crystals, talismans, or symbols that hold personal significance. Create altars or sacred spaces to meditate, reflect, or connect with your spiritual practice.

- **Ideal thinking and self-design:** Approach each room intentionally, considering how it serves your daily life and spiritual practice. Design your space to reflect your personality and aspirations and support your physical, emotional, and spiritual needs.

Bedroom Magic

The bedroom is a sanctuary for rest, rejuvenation, and intimate connection. Keep this space free from clutter and electronic distractions. Use soft lighting, calming colors, and natural materials to create a serene atmosphere. Incorporate elements that promote restful sleep and relaxation, such as lavender sachets, Himalayan salt lamps, and gentle music. Position your bed according to Feng Shui principles, ideally with a solid headboard against a wall, to ensure stability and security.

In your bedroom, focus on creating an ambiance of tranquility and love. Use soothing shades of blue, green, or lavender to paint the walls, inviting calmness and restful sleep. Place amethyst or rose quartz on your bedside table to enhance emotional healing and love. Hang dream catchers or moon phase artwork to connect with the ethereal energy of the night. Your bed should be a haven of comfort for mind and body, adorned with plush pillows and soft, breathable linens. Embrace the magic of nightly rituals, such as reading by candlelight or meditation, to transition peacefully into sleep.

Bathroom and Cleaning

A bathroom is a place of purification and renewal. Maintain cleanliness and organization, using natural and nontoxic products to enhance the space's purity. Include elements of water, such as fountains or seashells, to apply the cleansing energy. Use candles, essential oils, and soft towels to create a spa-like environment. Consider including plants that thrive in humid conditions, such as ferns or bamboo, to bring in natural energy.

Transform your bathroom into a sanctuary of cleansing and rejuvenation. Utilize white and blue tones to invoke purity and serenity. Decorate with accents of natural materials, containers, and mirrors to enhance the elements of flow and renewal. Keep eucalyptus branches in your shower to release invigorating and healing aromas when the steam rises. Include Himalayan salt lamps and essential oil diffusers to energetically cleanse and purify the space. Use rituals like salt baths and aromatherapy to cleanse your body and spirit, washing away the day's stress and negativity.

Sitting Rooms and Social Spaces

Sitting rooms and social spaces are used for gathering, relaxation, and connection. Create a welcoming and vibrant sitting room that encourages connection and joy. Arrange your furniture in a circular or semi-circular layout to foster conversation and interaction. Use warm, inviting colors like deep reds, oranges, and gold to stimulate energy and warmth. Include a fireplace or a cluster of candles to invoke the element of fire, bringing warmth and transformation to your social gatherings. Decorate with vibrant artwork, colorful cushions, and throws that reflect your personality and passions. Keep the space uncluttered and organized, ensuring a harmonious flow of energy.

Landings and Passageways

Transform your hallways and landings into magical passages that guide and inspire. Often overlooked, these areas are crucial for maintaining energy flow throughout your home. Keep these areas well-lit and free from clutter to prevent stagnation. Using light, airy colors can make these often narrow spaces feel open and inviting. Hang mirrors strategically to reflect light and expand the sense of space.

Decorate with art or meaningful objects that guide you from one area to the next, ensuring that these transitional spaces are inviting and harmonious. Use Inspirational quotes, spiritual symbols, or family photos that tell the story of your journey. Place small plants or crystals along the way to keep the energy flowing and vibrant. Consider adding soft lighting, such as fairy lights or sconces, to create a warm and welcoming atmosphere as you transition from one room to another.

Light and Its Uses

Natural light is the purest and most rejuvenating energy source for your home. Maximizing the influx of sunlight into your living spaces is essential to enhancing the flow of positive energy. Keep your windows clean and unobstructed to allow sunlight to flood your rooms. Use light, airy curtains or blinds that can be easily drawn back to invite more light in. Consider placing mirrors opposite windows to reflect and amplify natural light, creating a brighter and more open ambiance.

Include reflective surfaces like glass or polished metals to bounce light around the room. Skylights and large windows can also be added to maximize natural illumination. The sun's rays brighten your home and infuse it with vibrant, life-affirming energy that can uplift your spirit and invigorate your daily life.

- **Ambient lighting:** This is the general illumination of a room, often provided by ceiling fixtures, chandeliers, or wall sconces. Opt for soft, warm light to create a cozy and inviting atmosphere. Dimmable lights are particularly useful, allowing you to adjust the brightness to suit different activities and moods.

- **Task lighting:** Focused lighting is necessary for specific activities such as reading, cooking, or working. Desk lamps, under-cabinet lights, and pendant lights are excellent choices for task lighting. Ensure that these lights are bright enough to reduce eye strain but also harmonize with the overall lighting scheme of the room.

- **Accent lighting:** Highlighting particular areas or objects in your home, such as artwork, plants, or architectural features, can add a touch of magic. Use spotlights, LED strips, or fairy lights to create focal points and draw attention to the elements that bring you joy and inspiration.

- **Candlelight:** On the other hand, candlelight adds a timeless and mystical quality to any space. The flickering flame of a candle can create an atmosphere of warmth, romance, and tranquility. Use candles made of natural wax, such as beeswax or soy, to avoid releasing toxins into the air. Scented candles infused with essential oils can enhance the ambiance by filling the room with soothing or invigorating aromas.

Include and Delight in the Magic of Modernity

Modern technology can enhance the magic and functionality of your home. Digital elements, such as smart home devices and entertainment systems, can provide convenience, efficiency, and an added layer of enjoyment. However, it is essential to harmonize these elements so they do not dominate or disrupt the tranquil and mystical atmosphere you aim to create.

- **Smart lighting:** Smart lighting systems allow you to easily control the brightness, color, and timing of your lights. Use these systems to create dynamic lighting scenes that adapt to different times of the day or activities. In the evening, set your light to a warm, dim glow to unwind and prepare for restful sleep.

- **Smart home devices:** Smart home devices, such as voice-activated assistants, thermostats, and security systems, can enhance the comfort and safety of your home. Integrate these devices seamlessly into your environment by choosing designs that blend with your decor. Use them to automate mundane tasks, freeing your time and energy to focus on more meaningful and magical activities.

- **Balancing technology and nature:** Strive to balance the technological elements in your home with natural and spiritual elements. Surround your digital devices with plants, crystals, or natural textures to create a harmonious blend of modernity and nature. For example, place a beautiful quartz crystal next to your smart speaker to infuse the space with positive energy. Use wooden frames or shelves to house your tech gadgets, including the grounding energy of earth elements.

- **Digital detox zones:** Create areas where digital devices are not allowed in your home, creating spaces for unplugging and reconnecting with yourself and your loved ones. Designate rooms or corners for dedication, reading, or creative pursuits, free from the distractions of screens and notifications. These sanctuaries will serve as refuges where you can immerse yourself in the present moments and engage in spiritual practices.

Spell for Uplifting the Energy of Your Home

You will need

- a white candle (for purity and positive energy)
- a small bowl of water (representing emotion and intuition)
- a handful of salt (for grounding and protection)
- a sprig of fresh rosemary or sage (for wisdom and clarity)
- a crystal of your choice (for amplifying energy, such as clear quartz or amethyst)
- essential oils (lavender for calm, lemon for freshness, or peppermint for clarity)
- a piece of paper and a pen
- a small dish or bowl for the paper

Preparation

1. **Create your sacred space.** Choose a central location in your home where you can perform the spell undisturbed. This could be your living room, altar space, or any area where you feel comfortable and connected.

2. **Set up your altar.** Place the white candle, water bowl, salt, rosemary or sage, crystal, and essential oils on a table or flat surface. Arrange these items thoughtfully, as their energy will contribute to the spell.

3. **Ground and center yourself.** Sit comfortably and take three deep breaths, grounding yourself in the present moment. Visualize a protective circle of white light surrounding you and your space.

Steps

1. **Light the candle.** As you light the candle, cast the words, "A candle of white, pure, and bright, illuminate my home with your light. Cleanse the space, remove all blight, and fill it with love, joy, and delight."

2. **Bless the water.** Hold the water bowl in your hands and sprinkle a pinch of salt into it. String gently with your finger. As you do so, repeat the following: "Water and salt, pure and clear, cleanse this space, remove all fear. Emotion and protection intertwine and bring forth energies divine."

3. **Invoke the elements.** Take the rosemary or sage and wave it through the air, allowing its fragrance to cleanse the space. Repeat these words as you do this: "By earth and air, by fire and sea, balance and harmony come to be. In every room, bring forth beauty, love, and grace."

4. **Amplify with crystals.** Hold the crystal and close your eyes. Visualize its energy, amplifying the positive vibrations in your home. With your eyes closed, say, "Crystal clear and crystal bright, amplify this home with your light. Bring forth energy, pure and true, and infuse this space with all that's new."

5. **Add the essential oils:** Add a few drops of essential oil to the water bowl. Dip your fingers into the mixture and flick the water around each room as you walk through your home. While walking and flicking the water, repeat, "Oils of lavender, lemon, or mint will freshen the air with their fragrant hint.

Bring calm, clarity, and joy anew. Uplift this home in all we do."

6. **Write your intentions:** Hold the bowl with the paper and speak your intentions aloud. Visualize your home glowing with positive energy. Focusing on your energy, say, "By candle's light, crystal's gleam, herb and oil, salt and stream. I call forth energies bright and pure to bless this home always."

7. **Close the spell:** Extinguish the candle and thank the elements for their presence and assistance. You can thank them by repeating, "Elements of earth, air, fire, and sea, thank you for your gift to me. As I will, so shall it be; this home is blessed, so shall it be."

Walk through each room, feeling the uplifted energy and harmony you've created. Smile and take a moment to appreciate the beauty and balance of your magical home. Your sanctuary is now infused with positive vibrations, ready to support and nurture you on your spiritual journey.

Chapter 3:

Tending the Hearth

Clarity about what matters provides clarity about what does not. –Cal Newport

Living in your magical space requires mindfulness and care. Each action you take should be intentional, aimed at protecting and nourishing the energy you've so carefully cultivated. Regularly cleanse your space with smoke from sacred herbs like sage or cedar or use the sound vibrations from bells and chimes to dispel stagnant energy. Arrange your furniture and magical tools in ways that promote a harmonious flow of energy, reflecting the values you hold dear. Fresh flowers, bowls of fruit, and plants all signal your home is a living entity, a mirror of your inner self, and maintaining its sanctity is an ongoing practice of respect and devotion.

Sharing your magical space with others is both an art and a responsibility. When you invite guests into your home, think about how you want to present your space and the energy you wish to share. Create an inviting atmosphere with thoughtful touches like candles, music, and carefully prepared food.

Connection to the Magic of Nature and Higher Self

Witchcraft is about connecting to the magic of nature, your higher self, and something beyond—be it deity, spirit, or the universe. It's about being at one with your true self in all aspects of your life. This profound connection is the essence of witchcraft, guiding us to live in harmony with the natural world and our inner being.

When we step into our magical space, we are crossing a threshold into a physical area and a realm where the mundane and the mystical merge. Here, we attune ourselves to the whispers of the wind, the moon's phases, and the seasons' cycles. We become acutely aware of the energies that flow through all living things, recognizing that we are part of a vast, interconnected web of existence.

We cultivate a deeper relationship with our higher selves in this sacred space. Through mediation, ritual, and reflection, we peel back the layers of our consciousness, revealing the divine spark within. This journey inward is a path to self-discovery and empowerment, where we learn to trust our intuition and embrace our true potential. As we align with our higher self, we become more attuned to the guidance of spirits, deities, and the universe, opening ourselves to the wisdom and support they offer. This communion with the divine infuses our lives with meaning and purpose, helping us navigate the challenges and triumphs of our earthly journey with grace and clarity.

Cultural Traditions and Behaviors

We can be inspired and learn about the magic of our homes through other cultures. One beautiful tradition comes from Japan, where removing shoes before entering a home is more than just a custom—it is a spiritual practice. This ritual acknowledged the home as a sacred space, free from the impurities of the outside world. By leaving their shoes at the door, individuals symbolically cleanse themselves of the day's stress and negativity, ensuring that only pure, positive energy enters the living space.

In Italy, the "la dolce vita" concept extends into the home, where the focus is on creating an environment of warmth, beauty, and hospitality. Italian homes often feature a kitchen at their heart, where meals are prepared with love and shared with family and friends. This tradition emphasizes the home as a place of nourishment for the body and the soul.

In Native American cultures, smudging is used to cleanse and purify the home. This involves burning sacred herbs, such as sage or sweetgrass, and allowing the smoke to drift through each room. The smoke is believed to carry away negative energies, leaving the space cleansed and protected. This ritual is often accompanied by prayers or intentions, further imbuing the home with positive energy and spiritual protection.

Hygge, a Danish concept, focuses on creating a cozy, welcoming atmosphere in the home. It involves filling the space with soft lighting, comfortable furnishings, and elements of nature, such as plants and wood. Hygge is about finding joy in simple, everyday pleasures and creating an environment that fosters relaxation and contentment.

In Indian culture, the practice of "Vastu Shastra" is used to harmonize with the natural world. Similar to Feng Shui, Vastu Shastra involves arranging furniture, colors, and decor in a way that promotes positive energy flow. This ancient practice is based on the belief that our homes are a microcosm of the universe, and by aligning them with the principles of nature, we can create a space that supports our well-being and spiritual growth. Including elements of Vastu Shastra in our home can help us create a balanced, harmonious environment that nurtures our magical practices.

Sacred Spaces

One of the most powerful ways to create a sacred space is by setting up an altar. This can be a dedicated table or a small shelf adorned with items that hold spiritual significance. Add candles, crystals, herbs, and symbols that resonate with your practice. For instance, you might include a piece of amethyst for spiritual growth, a white candle for purity, and a small bowl of water to represent emotional depth and intuition. Spend time each day at your altar, lighting candles, meditating, or reflecting on your intentions. This practice grounds you and strengthens your connection to your spiritual path.

You can transform your bathroom into a sacred space for cleansing and renewal by using elements like sea salt, essential oils, and flowers in your bathwater to create a ritual bath. Lavender and chamomile can soothe your spirit, while rosemary and mint can invigorate your senses. Light candles and play sounds/soft music to enhance the atmosphere.

As you soak, visualize the water washing away negativity and replenishing you with positive energy.

Another sacred space, a cozy corner where you can retreat with a good book or journal, is a winner in any home. Choose a comfortable chair, add soft lighting, and surround yourself with inspiring items. This space can serve as your sanctuary for intellectual and emotional nourishment by including a small table for a cup of tea, a warm throw blanket, and perhaps a few crystals or plants to maintain a connection with nature.

Create sacred spaces in your home by infusing magic into everyday objects.

- **Crystals:** Crystals are powerful tools for channeling and amplifying energy. Place them around your home to enhance different areas. For example, keep rose quartz in your bedroom to promote love and harmony, or citrine in your workspace to encourage creativity and abundance. Clear quartz can be placed anywhere to amplify your home's overall energy. Arrange them in grids or clusters to magnify their power.

- **Herbs and plants:** Herbs and plants bring the magic of nature indoors. Hang bundles of dried herbs like sage, rosemary, or lavender in your kitchen for protection, clarity, and tranquility. Fresh plants, such as aloe vera and jade, can purify the air and attract prosperity. Each plant and herb carries its own unique energy, contributing to the overall harmony of your space.

- **Symbols and talismans:** Integrate symbols and talismans into your decor to serve as constant reminders of your intentions and beliefs. Hang a pentagram or a triple moon symbol near your entrance to ward off negative energy and invite positive vibes. Place a dreamcatcher above your bed to protect your sleep and encourage peaceful dreams. These symbols enhance your home's visual appeal and anchor its magical energy.

- **Sound:** Wind chimes, bells, and singing bowls can clear stagnant energy and raise the vibration of your home. Hang wind chimes near windows or doors to create a gentle, melodic sound whenever the wind blows, reminding you of the energy flowing through your space.

- **Essential oils:** Essential oils are potent tools for infusing your home with specific energies. Experiment and explore different oils like lavender for relaxation, eucalyptus for purification, or lemon to boost energy and positivity. Anoint doorways and windowsills with protective oil such as frankincense or rosemary to safeguard your space. You can also create sprays with diluted oils to cleanse and refresh the air in each room.

- **Personal touches:** Personalize these areas with items that have deep meaning. These can be family heirlooms, travel souvenirs, or handmade crafts. These personal touches infuse your home with your essence, making it a true sanctuary. For example, a cherished piece of jewelry passed down from a grandmother is placed on your altar as a symbol of ancestral guidance and protection. Or display a collection of seashells from a favorite beach trip to invoke the calm, vital energy of the sea.

The Sacred Hearth

The hearth is more than just a source of physical warmth—it is a wellspring of spiritual energy. It radiates heat and light, creating an inviting atmosphere that draws people in. This energy can be harnessed and directed to foster a sense of unity and purpose within your home. Consider the hearth a sacred altar where you can perform rituals, cook nourishing meals, and offer gratitude for the abundance in your life. Light a candle on your hearth each evening to invoke the eternal flame of love and protection. As you do so, recite a simple blessing or affirmation, inviting warmth and harmony into your home. This daily ritual anchors your intentions and strengthens the magical energy of your hearth.

The hearth has always been the heart of the home, where people gather to share meals, stories, and companionship. It is a place where bonds are strengthened and memories are made. By fostering this tradition, you cultivate a sense of belonging and connection for everyone who enters your home. Encourage gatherings around your hearth, whether it's a cozy fireplace, a kitchen stove, or a symbolic hearth created with candles and decorative elements. Invite family and friends to share stories and enjoy each other's company. This practice warms the body and nurtures the soul. Host a regular hearth night where loved ones gather to share their experiences, dreams, and challenges. Create a welcoming space with comfortable seating, soft lighting, and perhaps a pot of mulled wine or herbal tea. This tradition can become a cherished time of connection and support and will create memories.

This place is also a natural setting for teaching and storytelling. Throughout history, it has been a place where elders pass down wisdom and traditions to younger generations. Embrace this role by using your hearth to share knowledge, whether it's about your magical practice, family history, or life lessons. Gather around the hearth to tell stories, folk tales, personal experiences, or myths from various cultures. Storytelling entertains, teaches valuable lessons, and fosters a sense of continuity and connection. Light a fire or candle on a cold evening and invite everyone to share a favorite story. As each person speaks, the flickering flames enhance the magical ambiance and make the stories come alive.

For your "hearth night," imagine who you would invite and the warm energies they will bring. Prepare your hearth to envelop their love and presence, creating a space of warmth and protection. It's an opportunity to share stories, learn from one another, and deepen bonds in an environment imbued with care and intention.

Including magical elements in your hearth will enhance its sacred energy. Adorn it with symbols of protection, prosperity, and love. Use herbs, crystals, and candles to create a powerful, enchanted space that supports your intention and rituals. Place protective herbs like rosemary and sage on your hearth crystals, such as amethyst for spiritual growth or citrine for abundance. These elements amplify the hearth's energy and align it with your magical goals.

The Cauldron: History, Importance, and Symbolism Today

The cauldron is one of the most iconic symbols of witchcraft, steeped in history and rich with magical significance. Traditionally, the cauldron was a vessel for cooking and brewing potions, representing the transformative power of fire and the alchemical process. Wise women and witches used the cauldron to concoct herbal remedies, perform rituals, and even gaze into the future using water or fire.

Historically, the cauldron was an essential tool in every household, often large enough to cook a meal for an entire family. Over time, it took on a more symbolic role in witchcraft, representing the goddess's womb and the cyclical nature of life, death, and rebirth. In Celtic mythology, the cauldron of the goddess Cerridwen was a source of inspiration and knowledge, further cementing its place in magical practices.

Today, the cauldron remains a potent symbol of transformation and creation. Modern witches use cauldrons for various purposes, such as burning herbs, mixing potions, and conducting fire rituals. The cauldron's ability to hold and transform elements makes it a powerful tool in practical and symbolic magic.

Harnessing the Element of Fire Magic Safely

Fire is a dynamic and transformative element in witchcraft, embodying passion, energy, and purification. When working with fire, safety is paramount. Always use fireproof containers, keep water or a fire extinguisher nearby, and never leave a burning flame unattended.

Fire Purification Ritual

Fire can be used in various magical practices, from candle spells to bonfire rituals. It is particularly effective for spells involving transformation, purification, and energy.

You will need

- a small cauldron or fireproof bowl
- a piece of paper and a pen
- a red or white candle

Steps

1. Write down what you wish to preserve or release on paper.
2. Light the candle and focus on the flame, visualizing it as a source of cleansing energy.
3. Burn the paper in the cauldron, watching the flames consume your written intentions.
4. As the paper burns, say: "By fire's light and fire's might, cleanse and purify, set things right."

Candle Magic at Home—Spells by Light

Candles are a simple yet powerful tool in witchcraft. They represent the element of fire and are used to focus intent, send prayers, and cast spells. Candle magic is accessible and tailored to suit various needs and intentions. For this protection spell, we will use a white candle.

Protection Spell

Materials needed

- a white candle
- a piece of black cloth
- a pinch of salt
- a needle or pin

Steps

1. Carve a protective symbol (like a pentagram) into the candle using the needle.
2. Place the candle on a black cloth sprinkled with salt.
3. Light the candle and visualize a protective barrier surrounding you and your home.
4. Speak with intention: "Light of white, pure and bright, guard and protect through the night."

Incense and Oils—Domestic Ritual

Incense and oils are integral to many domestic rituals, providing a sensory experience that enhances the magical atmosphere. Incense, made from aromatic plant materials, is often burned to purify spaces, attract positive energy, and aid in meditation. Different types of incense are used for various purposes.

- **Sage:** Cleansing and purification
- **Lavender:** Calm and relaxation
- **Frankincense:** Spirituality and protection

Incense Cleansing Ritual

Materials needed

- a sage smudge stick or incense
- a fireproof dish

Steps

1. Light the sage smudge stick or incense.
2. Walk through your home, allowing the smoke to fill each room.
3. Focus on your intention to cleanse and purify the space.
4. Recite: "Smoke of sage, cleanse and clear, bring pure light and banish fear."

Love Anointing Oil

Essential oils can be used in various ways, including anointing candles, adding to baths, or diffusing the air. Each oil has its own magical properties.

Materials needed

- rose essential oil
- lavender essential oil
- a small glass bottle

Steps

1. Mix a few drops of rose and lavender oils in the glass bottle.
2. Anoint candles, pulse points, or objects with the oil to attract love and harmony.

Warmth, Comfort, and Protection Spells

Creating a warm and protective environment is crucial in maintaining a magical home. Spells and rituals that enhance warmth, comfort, and protection can make your home a sanctuary.

Materials needed

- a black candle
- a bowl of salt
- four small crystals (black tourmaline or obsidian)

Steps

1. Place the black candle in the center of your home.
2. Arrange the four crystals at the four corners of your home.
3. Sprinkle a circle of salt around the candle.
4. Light the candle and speak to the room: "By the power of earth and flame, I protect this home in my name."

Eating by Candlelight

Eating by candlelight can transform mealtime into a magical ritual. Replace the TV with a warm glow of candles and engage in storytelling to foster connection and mindfulness.

1. Set the table with candles, one for each person.
2. Before eating, light the candles and each share a story or something you're grateful for.
3. Enjoy your meal in the soft, magical light, focusing on the flavors and the company.

Nurturing Relationships With Hearth Magic

The hearth is a powerful symbol of home and family and it can be used to nurture relationships. Simple rituals and spells performed around the hearth can strengthen bonds and create harmony.

Materials needed

- a pink candle

- a bowl of rose petals

a small piece of paper and a pen

Steps

1. Write the names of your family members on the paper.

2. Light the pink candle and place it in the bowl of rose petals.

3. Place the paper under the candle.

4. Position the candle near your hearth or a symbolic representation of it.

5. Visualize love and harmony filling your home as the candle burns.

6. Say: "Love and light, peace and grace, fill this home, bless this space."

Welcoming Guests With Warmth and Blessings

When inviting guests into your home, it is important to create a welcoming atmosphere that reflects your magical intentions. Simple rituals can set a positive tone and ensure guests feel honored and respected.

Materials needed

- a white candle
- a bowl of fresh flowers
- a small dish of salt

Steps

1. Light the white candle at the entrance of your home.
2. Place the bowl of flowers and the dish of salt nearby.
3. As guests arrive, invite them to take a pinch of salt and sprinkle it into the bowl of flowers, symbolizing their wish for a joyful visit.
4. Say: "Welcome to my home, and with light and love, may we share the blessings of this evening together."

Creating a Peaceful Environment for Disagreements

Disagreements and conflicts are natural but can be navigated with grace by creating a peaceful environment. Using elements of hearth magic, you can facilitate understanding and resolution.

Materials needed

- a blue candle
- a bowl of water
- a few drops of lavender oil

Steps

1. Light the blue candle and place it in front of the water bowl.

2. Add the drops of lavender oil to the water.

3. As you and the other person(s) sit near the candle and water, visualize the calming energy of the water and lavender, soothing tempers and fostering understanding.

4. Set your intention and say these words silently or into the room: "Water calm, fire bright, bring peace and resolution tonight."

Home Magic for Love and Friendship

Simple but effective magical practices can enhance love and friendship within your home. These spells and rituals strengthen bonds and invite loving energy into your space.

Materials needed

- a pink candle
- a small piece of rose quartz
- a bowl of honey

Steps

1. Light the pink candle and place the rose quartz in the bowl of honey.

2. Visualize the sweetness of honey, attracting and strengthening friendships.

3. Dip your finger into the honey, touch the rose quartz, and then touch your heart.

4. Speak with intention: "Sweet as honey, strong as stone, may our friendships always grow.

Embrace these practices with an open heart, and let the warmth and light of your hearth guide you on your magical journey. Continue on the journey with me to the next chapter, where we'll list spells and rituals to create a magical home and guide you to clean your spaces with love and protection.

Chapter 4:

Recipes, Spells, and Rituals to Create a Magical Home

This chapter is your recipe book—a collection of carefully crafted rituals designed to infuse your home with the spiritual energy, harmony, and protection described in the previous chapters. From grounding and meditative practices to practical cleansing and purification techniques, these spells will help you manifest the sanctuary you envision.

List of Elements and Materials for Casting Spells and Performing Rituals

An enchanted home involves the thoughtful use of different elements and materials, each with its own unique properties and significance. This section provides a comprehensive list of essential items you'll need to cast spells and perform rituals, ensuring that your practices are effective and meaningful.

Elements

- **Fire**
    - candles
    - incense sticks or cones

- o matches or lighters
- o fireproof dishes
- **Water**
    - o bowls for water
    - o sea salt or Himalayan salt
    - o essential oils
    - o herbal infusions
- **Earth**
    - o crystals and gemstones
    - o soil or sand
    - o herbs, dried and fresh
    - o plants and flowers
- **Air**
    - o feathers
    - o bells and chimes
    - o incense
    - o wind chimes
- **Spirit**
    - o personal talismans
    - o symbols (pentagrams, runes)
    - o altar items

- spiritual icons or statues

Materials for Spells and Rituals

- **Candles**
    - White: Purity, protection, spiritual growth
    - Red: Passion, strength, love
    - Green: Prosperity, health, and abundance
    - Blue: Peace, healing, communication
    - Purple: Intuition, psychic abilities, wisdom
    - Black: Banishing, protection, grounding
- **Crystals and gemstones**
    - Amethyst: Spiritual growth, protection
    - Rose Quartz: Love, harmony, and emotional healing
    - Clear Quartz: Amplification, clarity, and healing
    - Citrine: Prosperity, creativity, abundance
    - Black tourmaline: Protection, grounding, and banishing negativity
- **Herbs and plants**
    - Sage: Cleansing, purification
    - Lavender: Calm, relaxation, peace
    - Rose: Love, harmony, and emotional balance
    - Eucalyptus: Cleansing, protection, healing

- Lemon: Freshness, clarity, positivity

- **Incense**
    - Frankincense: Spirituality, protection
    - Myrrh: Healing, purification
    - Sandalwood: Meditation, grounding
    - Cedar: Protection, cleansing
    - Patchouli: Prosperity, grounding

- **Altar tools**
    - Cauldron: Transformation, brewing, and fire rituals
    - Athame: Direction of energy, cutting through negativity
    - Wand: Channeling energy, directing intention
    - Chalice: Water element, offerings, emotional healing
    - Pentacle: Protection, grounding, representing the earth's element

- **Other spiritual items**
    - Feathers: Air element, communication, spiritual connection
    - Bells and chimes: Sound cleansing, energy raising
    - Mortar and pestle: Grinding herbs, creating potions
    - Jars and bottles: Storing potions, herbs, and oils
    - Personal talismans: Objects imbued with personal power and intention

Spiritual Practices: Listening to the Voice of Your Home

Creating a balanced connection at home goes beyond the physical arrangement of objects; it involves tuning into the spiritual energy of your space and connecting deeply with your inner self. Always remember to start with yourself. Spiritual practices help you listen for guidance, understand your true needs, and hear the voice of your home.

Asking for Guidance Ritual

Asking for guidance from the spiritual intuitive realm is a foundational practice in witchcraft. Whether you are calling upon deities, spirit guides, or universal energy, asking for guidance can provide clarity and direction.

Materials needed

- a purple candle
- a piece of amethyst
- a small bowl of water
- lavender essential oil

Steps

1. Find a quiet area where you won't be disturbed. Light the purple candle, place the amethyst and bowl of water in front of you, and add a few drops of lavender oil to the water.

2. Sit comfortably and close your eyes. Take deep, calming breaths, and let go of any tension or distractions.

3. Focus on your question or the guidance you seek. Speak your intention aloud, asking your chosen spiritual guides for their wisdom and insight.

4. Spend a few moments in silence, listening for any messages or feelings that come to you. Trust that the guidance will manifest in some form, whether a thought, a feeling, or a sudden clarity.

5. Thank your guides for their presence, and extinguish the candle. Reflect on any insights you receive and write them down in your journal.

Looking Inward Ritual

Self-reflection is a powerful tool for understanding your true desires and needs. By looking inward, you can better understand your emotions, motivations, and spiritual path.

Materials needed

- a journal
- a pen
- a comfortable, quiet space

Steps

1. Sit in a comfortable, quiet place to focus without interruptions.

2. Start writing about your current feelings, thoughts, and experiences in your journal. Allow your thoughts to flow freely without judgment.

3. Pose questions to yourself, such as "What do I truly desire?" or "What is my purpose?" Write down your answers and reflect on them.

4. Spend a few minutes in meditation, focusing on your breath and allowing any insights to surface. Write down any revelations or important thoughts that come to you.

Listening to the Voice of Our Home

Every home has a unique spirit and energy that can guide us in creating a harmonious and balanced environment.

Materials needed

- a white candle
- a piece of selenite
- a small bowl of water
- a few drops of rosemary essential oil

Steps

1. Light the white candle and place the selenite and bowl of water nearby. Add a few drops of rosemary oil to the water.

2. Sit quietly and close your eyes. Take deep breaths and focus on the energy of your home. Imagine a white light spreading throughout each room, filling your home with positive energy.

3. With your eyes closed, focus on your home's subtle sounds and sensations. What do you feel? What do you hear? Pay attention to any impressions or thoughts that arise.

4. Speak around your home, expressing your intention to create a harmonious and loving environment. Ask your home to guide you in making it a sanctuary of peace and magic.

5. Open your eyes and spend a few moments reflecting on any insight or feelings that came to you. Write them down in your journal for future reference.

Morning Ritual

This ritual combines elements of grounding, intention-setting, and spiritual protection to help you face the day with confidence and grace.

Materials needed

- a yellow or white candle
- a piece of clear quartz or citrine
- a small bowl of water
- a few drops of lemon or peppermint essential oil.

Steps

1. Choose a quiet spot where you can perform this ritual undisturbed. Light the yellow or white candle to represent the new day's energy and place the clear quartz or citrine nearby.

2. Sit comfortably and place your feet firmly on the ground. Close your eyes and take several deep breaths, imagining roots growing from your feet into the earth, grounding and stabilizing yourself.

3. Hold the clear quartz or citrine in your hands. Focus on your intention for the day—whether it's to be productive, stay calm, or attract positive energy. Visualize your intention clearly and feel it resonate within you.

4. Add a few drops of lemon or peppermint essential oil to the water bowl. Dip your fingers into the water and lightly sprinkle it around your space, saying: "With this water, pure and bright, I cleanse myself with morning light."

5. Hold the crystal close to your heart and recite an affirmation that aligns with your intentions, such as: "I am focused, I am strong, and I attract positivity all day long." Visualize a protective light surrounding you, shielding you from negativity.

6. Spend a few moments in silence, feeling the energy you've created. Blow out the candle, thanking it for its light and protection. Carry the crystal throughout the day as a reminder of your intention.

Enchanting Ritual for the Evening

This ritual focuses on releasing the day's stress, inviting tranquility, and setting intentions for a peaceful night.

Materials needed

- a blue or lavender candle
- a piece of amethyst or moonstone
- a small bowl of salt water
- a few drops of lavender or chamomile essential oil

Steps

1. Find a serene spot in your home where you can relax. Light the blue or lavender candle to represent the calming energy of the evening. Place the amethyst or moonstone nearby.

2. Sit comfortably and close your eyes. Take deep breaths, focusing on releasing tension or stress from the day. Imagine a wave of calm washing over you, cleansing away worries.

3. Hold the amethyst or moonstone in your hands. Reflect on your intention for the evening—whether to rest peacefully, dream vividly, or simply relax. Visualize this intention.

4. Add a few drops of lavender or chamomile essential oil to the bowl of salt water. Dip your fingers into the water and sprinkle it around your space, saying: "With this water, salt, and oil, I invite peace, free from toil."

5. Hold the crystal close to your heart and recite an affirmation that aligns with your evening intention, such as: "I am calm, I am at peace. I welcome rest and sweet release." Visualize a serene light enveloping you, promoting relaxation and peaceful sleep.

6. Spend a few moments in silence, absorbing your cultivated tranquility. Blow out your candle, thanking it for its calming presence. Place the crystal under your pillow or bedside table to enhance restful sleep.

Practical Rituals for Cleaning and Spiritual Purification

Maintaining a mystical home involves regular practices that cleanse and purify the physical and energetic space within. These practical rituals ensure your home remains a sanctuary of positive energy and spiritual harmony. In this section, we will explore each room's methods and steps for effective cleansing, smudging, and spiritual purification.

Cleaning Ritual

A clean home is the foundation of a magical environment. Physical cleaning removes dust and dirt, while energetic cleaning removes negative or stagnant energy.

Materials needed

- a broom or vacuum
- cleansing cloths
- natural cleaning solutions (vinegar, baking soda, lemon)
- a small bowl of salt

- a white candle

Steps

1. Before cleaning, light the white candle and set your intentions. Set small bowls of salt in the corners of the home or room. Visualize your home filled with bright, positive energy and say, "As I clean, I clear away negativity and make space for light and positivity."

2. Start by physically cleaning your home. Dust, sweep, mop, and vacuum each room. Use natural cleaning solutions like vinegar and lemon for a fresh and pure environment. A Basil oil and water mop of your hard floors seals your energies into your home.

3. Sprinkle a small amount of salt in each corner of the room to absorb negative energy. Allow the salt to sit while you continue cleaning.

4. After cleaning, gather the salt from each corner and dispose of it outside your home. Visualize any absorbed negativity leaving your space.

5. Thank the white candle for its light and protection, then blow it out.

Smudging Ritual

Smudging is a powerful practice for purifying the air and energy in your home. It involves burning sacred herbs to cleanse and uplift the environment.

Materials needed

- a sage smudge stick or palo santo
- a fireproof dish

- a feather or fan

Steps

1. Open windows and doors to allow negative energy to escape. Light the sage smudge stick, or palo santo, and let it smolder, producing smoke.

2. Focus on your intention to cleanse and purify. Say: "Smoke of sage (or palo santo), cleanse and clear, bring pure light and banish fear."

3. Walk through each room, allowing the smoke to reach every corner. Use a feather or fan to direct the smoke, if desired. Pay special attention to doorways, windows, and corners where energy can stagnate.

4. As you smudge, visualize the smoke lifting away any negative or stagnant energy, leaving a bright, clear space behind.

5. Once you've smudged the entire home, extinguish the smudge stick in the fireproof dish. Take a moment to appreciate the renewed energy of your space.

Spiritual Purification of Each Room

Purifying each room spiritually involves invoking the elements and using symbolic gestures to bless and protect the space.

Materials needed

- a small bowl of water
- sea salt or Himalayan salt
- a feather
- a candle (white or any color that resonates with your intention)

- incense (frankincense or sandalwood)

Steps

1. Light the candle and incense, placing them in the central location in your purifying room.

2. Invoke and acknowledge each element.

    - Earth: Sprinkle a pinch of salt in each corner of the room.

    - Water: Dip your fingers in the water bowl and flick a few drops in each corner.

    - Air: Wave the feather in each corner, stirring the air and symbolizing clarity.

    - Fire: Carry the lit candle around the room, visualizing the flame burning away and negativity

3. Stand in the center of the room and close your eyes. Focus on your intention to purify and bless the space. Speak slowly and say: "By the power of earth, water, air, and fire, I cleanse and bless this space. May it be filled with light, love, and positive energy."

4. As you say these words, visualize the room with a bright, purifying light. Feel the energy shift, becoming lighter and more vibrant.

5. Move from room to room, repeating these steps to purify the entire home spiritually.

6. Return to the central location once you have purified each room. Thank the elements for their assistance and extinguish the candle and incense.

Rituals to Recognize the Sanctity of Each Space

Each room in your home holds a unique energy and purpose. Recognizing and honoring the sanctity of each space is essential to maintaining a harmonious and spiritually vibrant environment. By performing rituals and meditations, you can enhance the sacredness of your home and align it with your intentions and values.

Creating sacred spaces includes more than just physical arrangement; it requires understanding the room's purpose and how it fits into your life. For example, your bedroom is a place of rest and rejuvenation, your kitchen is for nourishment and creativity, and your living room is for socializing and relaxation. Each space should be treated with the respect and intention it deserves.

Bedroom Sanctification Ritual

Materials needed

- a blue candle

- a small bowl of lavender water (mix water with a few drops of lavender essential oil)

- a piece of rose quartz

Steps

1. Tidy your bedroom, ensuring it is clean and clutter-free.

2. Light the blue candle on your bedside table, setting a calm and peaceful atmosphere.

3. Dip your fingers in the lavender water and lightly sprinkle it around the room, particularly on your bed. As you do this, speak to the room: "Lavender water, pure and bright, brings peace and calm through the night."

4. Sit on your bed and hold the rose quartz. Close your eyes and take deep breaths, feeling the soothing energy of the crystal. Visualize your bedroom as a sanctuary of rest and healing.

5. Recite an affirmation: "This room is a sanctuary of peace and rest. I am safe, I am loved, and I am rejuvenated here."

6. Let the candle burn for a few more minutes as you sit silently, absorbing the calm energy. Then, extinguish the candle and place the rose quartz on your bedside table.

Grounding and Meditative Practices

Grounding and meditative practices help you connect with your home's energy and enhance its sanctity. Grounding meditations are essential for connecting to the earth and the present moment. They help stabilize your energy and anchor your intentions.

Steps

1. Choose a room or corner where you feel comfortable and won't be disturbed.

2. Sit with your feet flat on the floor. Close your eyes and take a few deep breaths.

3. Imagine roots growing from the soles of your feet, extending deep into the earth. Feel the stability and strength of these roots anchoring you.

4. With each breath, draw up energy from the earth through your roots, filling your body with grounding, stabilizing energy.

5. Continue breathing deeply, focusing on the sensation in your body and the connection to the earth. Spend at least five minutes in this state.

Practical Rituals for Cleansing

Practical rituals for cleansing your space help maintain its sanctity by removing negative energy and inviting positive vibrations. Perform these rituals regularly to keep your home energetically clean.

Daily Blessing Ritual

A simple daily blessing can keep the energy in your home positive and welcoming.

Steps

1. Light a small candle every morning and walk through each room, holding the candle in front of you.

2. As you move through your home, say a simple blessing: "May this home be filled with light, love, and peace. May all who enter feel welcomed and blessed."

3. Spend a moment in each room, visualizing it as filled with bright, positive energy.

4. After blessing each room, return to your starting point and extinguish the candle, thanking it for its light.

Recognizing and Honoring Each Space—Kitchen Blessing

Recognizing and honoring each space involves acknowledging its unique purpose and ensuring it aligns with your spiritual and practical needs. This can be achieved through thoughtful arrangement, regular cleansing, and specific rituals tailored to the room's function.

The kitchen is the heart of the home, where nourishment and creativity flow. A kitchen blessing ritual can enhance these qualities.

Materials needed

- a green candle

- a small bowl of herbs (basil, thyme, and rosemary)

Steps

1. Start by ensuring your kitchen is clean and organized.

2. Place the green candle in a central location in your kitchen and light it.

3. Sprinkle the herbs around your kitchen, particularly near your cooking area. As you do this, say, "Herbs of green, bless this space, bring nourishment and creativity to this place."

4. Visualize your kitchen filled with the energy of abundance and health. Imagine that the meals you prepare nourish you and your loved ones.

5. Let the candle burn for a while longer as you cook or prepare food, absorbing the blessing's energy. Then, extinguish the candle.

Energy Maintenance

Maintaining energy throughout your home is essential for creating a harmonious and spiritually vibrant environment. Just as you tend to the physical aspects of your home, such as cleaning and organizing, it's equally important to tend to its energetic aspects. Here are some magical practices to help you maintain energy throughout your home:

- **Regular cleansing rituals:** Remove any stagnant or negative energy from your home. This can be as simple as burning sage or palo santo and wafting the smoke throughout each room, paying special attention to corners and doorways where energy tends to accumulate. You can also use sounds like bells or singing bowls to cleanse and purify the space.

- **Recharging crystals:** If you have crystals placed throughout your home for their energetic properties, remember to recharge them regularly. You can do this by placing them in direct sunlight or moonlight for a few hours or burying them in the earth for a day or two. Visualize the crystals being cleansed and recharged with fresh, vibrant energy.

- **Setting intentions:** Set intentions for the energy you want to cultivate in your home. Before beginning any cleaning or organizing tasks, take a moment to center yourself and visualize your home filled with positive, uplifting energy. You can also infuse your cleansing products with essential oils or herbs that correspond to your intentions, such as lemon for purification or lavender for peace and tranquility.

- **Creating sacred spaces:** Designate specific areas in your home as sacred spaces where you can connect with the divine and recharge your energy. This could be a meditation corner with cushions and candles, an altar with meaningful objects and symbols, or even a cozy reading nook where you can escape and unwind. Spend time in these spaces regularly to recharge and rejuvenate your spirit.

- **Energetic boundaries:** Establish energetic boundaries to protect your home from unwanted influences or instructions. Visualize a protective bubble or shield surrounding your home, allowing only love and positive energy to enter while repelling negativity. For added protection, you can also place protective symbols, such as a pentacle or Hamsa, near your doors and windows.

Now that you have mastered the art of maintaining energy throughout your home, it is time to delve deeper into one of the most ethereal and essential areas of your living spaces: the hearth and kitchen. These spaces are the heartbeats of your home, where nourishment, warmth, and connections come together. In ancient times, the hearth was a sacred place, a source of physical sustenance and spiritual nourishment.

In the next chapter, "Magic of the Hearth and Kitchen," we will explore the rich traditions and practices that make these areas so special. From the art of kitchen witchery to rituals that enhance family bonds and prosperity, you will discover how to infuse your cooking and daily routines with intention and magic.

Chapter 5:

Magic of the Hearth and Kitchen

Your kitchen is the heart of your magical home, where the warmth of the hearth and the nourishing energy of the kitchen come together to create a powerful center of love, abundance, and spiritual growth. The kitchen is not merely a place for preparing meals; it is a sacred space where intuition and wisdom are blended daily. From the alchemical process of cooking to the rituals of gathering and sharing food, the kitchen is a pivotal area that sustains and enriches our lives.

The Power and History of the Kitchen Space

Historically, the kitchen has always been the heart of the home. In ancient times, the hearth was a central feature, providing warmth, light, and a place to cook food. Families gathered around the hearth to share stories, celebrate, and connect. This tradition continues today, as the kitchen remains a place of gathering and nourishment. The fire of the hearth symbolizes the life force energy that sustains us, making the kitchen a powerful spiritual and practical hub.

Here, we perform the simple yet profound acts of cooking and eating, transforming raw ingredients into nourishing meals that fuel our bodies and spirits. The magic of the kitchen lies in its ability to bring people together, provide comfort and sustenance, and serve as a space where intentions and rituals can be implemented into daily life.

Setting up Your Kitchen With Spirit

To harness the full potential of your kitchen's special energy, setting it up with intention and care is essential. Begin by cleansing the space, both physically and energetically. Use natural cleaning products to remove dirt and grime, and perform a smudging ritual with sage or palo santo to clear any negative energy. Open windows and doors to allow fresh air to circulate, bringing in new, vibrant energy.

Next, create a kitchen shrine to honor the life force energy of the hearth. This can be a small altar on a countertop or a dedicated shelf. Adorn your shrine with items that symbolize nourishment, abundance, and protection. Consider including candles, crystals, herbs, and symbols.

Infuse your kitchen with elements of the four directions and their corresponding energies. Place a bowl of water in the west to symbolize intuition and emotion; a bowl of salt or soil in the north for grounding and stability; a feather in the east to represent air and clarity of thought; and a small candle in the south for fire and transformation.

Kitchen History and How It Has Evolved to Today

The kitchen, often referred to as the heart of the home, has undergone significant transformations throughout history. In ancient times, the hearth was the central feature of any dwelling. It provided warmth, a place to cook food, and a gathering spot for families. In many cultures, the hearth was seen as the domain of goddesses, such as Hestia in Greek mythology or Brigid in Celtic lore, who was believed to preside over the household's well-being and prosperity.

As societies evolved, so did the kitchen. During the medieval period, large houses and castles had grand kitchens where food was prepared for the entire household. These kitchens were bustling centers of activity, often located away from living quarters to reduce the fire risk. The open hearth continued to be a vital element, with cauldrons and spits used for cooking.

With the Industrial Revolution, the kitchen began to transform into a more modern space we recognize today. Introducing stoves, ovens, and other appliances brought convenience and efficiency, changing the dynamics of kitchen work. By the 20th century, the kitchen had become more compact and integrated into the home's living space, reflecting the changing roles of family and work life. The open-concept design of modern homes further integrated the kitchen with dining and living areas, making it a central hub for social interaction.

Today, the kitchen is a blend of functionality and aesthetics. It is equipped with modern appliances, designed for convenience, and often serves as a space for both cooking and entertaining. Despite these changes, the kitchen remains a place of nourishment and connection, continuing its historical role as the heart of the home.

Your Feelings About Kitchen Work

Before fully reclaiming your kitchen as a magical and spiritual space, exploring your feelings about kitchen work is essential. Understanding your relationship with this environment is key to transforming it into a place of positive energy and purpose.

To reclaim your kitchen as a sacred space, reflect on whether you see it as a chore or a creative outlet. Consider the memories that shape your perception of the kitchen. Perhaps your perception is influenced by joyful memories of baking with family mixed with memories of stressful meal preparations. Here is a journaling exercise you can try:

- Find a quiet spot and light a candle or incense for a calming atmosphere.

- Close your eyes, take deep breaths, and think about your kitchen experiences.

- What emotions come up?

- Write honestly about your relationship with kitchen tasks. Exploring what brings you joy or frustration.

- Identify any recurring patterns or dominant feelings, and approach your kitchen with mindfulness and intention, creating a space for spiritual nourishment and magic.

Renewing Our Magical Kitchen Practices

Reclaiming your kitchen as a space for magic and spirituality entails practical and energetic steps. This process allows you to infuse your daily routines with intention and create a sacred environment where nourishment and spirituality coexist.

1. **Cleanse and declutter:** Begin by thoroughly cleaning your kitchen. Remove any clutter, expired food, and items that no longer serve you. As you clean, visualize removing stagnant energy and making space for positive vibrations. Use natural cleaning products like vinegar, lemon, and baking soda to purify the space physically.

2. **Energetic cleansing ritual:** Perform an energetic cleansing to rid the space of any lingering negativity. Light a sage smudge stick or palo santo and walk through your kitchen, allowing the smoke to reach every corner. Pay special attention to the stove and countertops, as these are areas where transformation (cooking) occurs. As you smudge, say your rituals.

3. **Infuse your cooking with intention:** Transform cooking into a magical practice by infusing your food with intention and positive energy. As you prepare meals, focus on the love and nourishment you are creating. Stir clockwise to invite prosperity and abundance and counterclockwise to banish negativity. Use herbs and spices for their flavor and their magical properties as well. When preparing a meal, take a moment to set your intention. Hold your hands over the ingredients and visualize them being filled with positive energy.

4. **Sacred mealtime rituals:** Create rituals around mealtime to enhance the sacredness of your kitchen. Light a candle before meals, say a blessing or gratitude prayer, and encourage mindful eating. These practices help transform ordinary meals into

moments of spiritual connection and reflection. Before eating, light a candle at the center of your table and hold hands with the present. Remember to say your ritual.

Kitchen Shrines and Altars

Creating a kitchen shrine or altar is a beautiful way to infuse your cooking space with spiritual energy and intention. Here's how you can set up your kitchen shrine:

1. **Choose the location.** Find a spot in your kitchen that is easily accessible and slightly out of the way so it won't be disturbed during daily activities. A windowsill, a small shelf, or a corner of your countertop can work perfectly.

2. **Select sacred items.** Adorn your shrine with items that resonate with your spiritual practice and symbolize nourishment, protection, and abundance. Here are some suggestions:

    o Candles represent the element of fire and the warmth of the hearth. Choose colors that align with your intentions.

    o Crystals are stones like citrine for abundance, rose quartz for love, and clear quartz for amplification. Place these crystals around your shrine to enhance its energy.

    o Herbs and spices, whether fresh or dried, like basil, rosemary, and thyme, can be placed in small jars or bowls. They look beautiful and bring their magical properties into the space.

    o Include symbols and talisman items such as a pentacle, a small deity statue, a beloved family heirloom, or other meaningful symbols.

- Leave small offerings, such as a bowl of fresh fruit, a cup of water, or a dish of salt, to honor the divine and express gratitude.

3. **Personalize your shrine.** This space should reflect your connection to the divine and the hearth. Add items that inspire you, such as inspirational quotes, pictures of loved ones, or anything that brings you joy and peace.

4. **Consecrate your shrine.** Once you have set up your shrine, consecrate it with a simple blessing. Light a candle and incense, and say: "Sacred space, blessed be, with love and light, I honor thee. May this hearth be ever bright, filled with magic day and night."

Using the Elements to Create Spells and Spiritual Foods

Our kitchen is a place where we transform gifts of ingredients into nourishment and sustenance that eventually become our bodies. By being mindful of these elements, you can enhance your magical practices and infuse your food with spiritual energy.

- **Fire:** Fire transforms raw ingredients into meal transformation and passion. When cooking, focus on the flame's power and visualize it energizing your food.

- **Water:** Water is essential for cooking and cleaning, symbolizing intuition and emotion. As you wash vegetables or boil water, infuse it with positive intentions, imagining it carrying your blessings throughout the meal.

- **Earth:** Earth provides the ingredients we use. Herbs, vegetables, and grains connect us to the earth's nurturing energy. Handle these ingredients with respect and gratitude, acknowledging their journey from the earth to your kitchen.

- **Air:** Air circulates the scents and flavors of your cooking. Use air to carry your prayers and intentions. Speak blessings into the air as you cook, and use gentle breaths to cool and bless hot dishes.

An Example of Elemental Cooking Meditation

- Before you start cooking, take a moment to acknowledge the elements in your kitchen.

- Representing fire, place it on your kitchen shrine.

- Connect with the element of air by taking a few deep breaths.

- Hold each ingredient and silently thank the earth and water for their growth and nourishment.

As you prepare your meal, focus on the elements at work and the magical energy they bring. Visualize your intentions being absorbed by the food.

Slow Down: The Magic Is in the Detail

In life, it's easy to rush through tasks without much thought. However, true magic lies in the details and the mindful presence we bring to our work. Slowing down allows us to connect deeply with our actions and infuse them with intention and spirituality.

Practicing Mindfulness in the Kitchen

1. Begin by creating a calming atmosphere. Light a candle or some incense, play soft music, and take a few moments to breathe and center yourself before you start your tasks.

2. Pay attention to your kitchen's sights, sounds, smells, and textures. Notice the colors of your ingredients, the sound of

chopping, the aroma of spices, and the feel of kneading dough. Engaging our senses fully helps us stay present and connected.

3. Be deliberate with your movements. Move slowly and intentionally, whether you are stirring a pot, chopping vegetables, or washing dishes. Visualize each action contributing to the overall energy of your home.

4. Express gratitude for the ingredients you use, the tools that aid you, and the nourishment you create. A simple "thank you" to the universe, the earth, and the food can transform your kitchen work into a spiritual practice.

5. Turn mundane tasks into rituals. For example, when you stir a pot, do so clockwise to invite positive energy and counterclockwise to release negativity. Use affirmations and mantras as you work, such as: "As I stir, I weave magic. As I cook, I nourish my soul."

Dishwashing Ritual

1. Light a candle and place it near the sink.

2. Take a deep breath and center yourself, focusing on the task at hand.

3. As you wash each dish, express gratitude for the meal it held and the nourishment it provided.

4. Visualize the water, cleansing the physical dish and any lingering negative energy, leaving it purified and ready for future use.

5. When you finish, take a moment to reflect on the nourishment and love you have infused into your kitchen.

The kitchen, with its blend of elements and daily rituals, becomes a powerful place where the mundane tasks of cooking and cleaning are elevated to the act of magic and mindfulness. By creating kitchen shrines, being mindful of the elements, and slowing down to appreciate the details, you turn our kitchen into the true heart of your home, infused with warmth, love, and spiritual energy.

Now that you have established this magical environment, it is time to delve deeper into the practices of kitchen craft and the spirituality and gift of food. In the next chapter, we will explore how food is more than just sustenance; it is a medium for spiritual expression, healing, and connection.

Chapter 6:

Kitchencraft and the Gift of Food

This chapter will guide you in transforming your kitchen into a place where every meal becomes a magical experience infused with intention, love, and gratitude. We will uncover how cooking can be a conduit for spiritual expression, healing, and connection. By being mindful of the ingredients you use, the methods you employ, and the emotions you bring to the process, you can create meals that nourish the body and the soul.

Kitchencraft and the Spirituality and Gift of Food

When it comes to offering food and drink to ourselves and others, it is crucial to first examine our inner environment. The state of our mind and spirit significantly influences the energy we infuse into our meals. Preparing food from a place of stress, anger, or distraction can unintentionally transfer these negative vibrations into the food. Conversely, cooking from a space of calm, love, and gratitude can enhance the nourishment and positive energy that the food provides.

Begin by centering yourself before you start cooking. Take a few deep breaths and clear your mind of any clutter. Set a clear intention for the meal you are about to prepare, focusing on the well-being and enjoyment of those who will eat it. Visualize the food absorbing this positive energy, transforming each ingredient into a vessel of love and nourishment. Here are the steps for the centering exercise:

1. Before you start preparing your meal, take a moment to sit quietly.

2. Close your eyes and take several deep breaths, inhaling calm and exhaling tension.

3. Think about the purpose of the meal—whether it's to nourish, celebrate, or heal. Hold this intention in your mind and let it guide your actions.

The Spirit of Generosity

Offering food and drink to ourselves and others is an act of generosity and care. It is a way to honor our shared connections and express love and gratitude. When we prepare food with a generous spirit, we nourish the body and feed the soul.

Gratitude is a powerful force that can transform cooking into a sacred ritual. As you prepare your ingredients, take a moment to express thanks for each one. Acknowledge the journey of the food from the earth to the kitchen, and give thanks for the nourishment it provides. Here are the steps for the gratitude ritual:

1. Take a piece of fruit, a vegetable, or any ingredient you use and hold it in your hands.

2. Think about where it came from, the farmers, the soil, and the journey to reach you.

3. Silently or aloud, say a few words of thanks for its nourishment and the energy it will provide.

Creating Offerings With Love

When making food and drink offerings, it's essential to infuse them with love and positive energy. This transforms the food into more than sustenance; it becomes a gift imbued with your best intentions and feelings.

As you cook, visualize the energy of love flowing from your hands into the food. Stir with intention, chop with care, and season with joy. Each action becomes a part of the offering, adding layers of positive energy. Here are the steps for the love infusion technique:

1. Imagine a warm, glowing light in your heart, radiating love.

2. Visualize this light flowing down your arms and into your hands as you cook.

3. Imagine this loving energy transferring into the food with each touch and movement.

Sharing the Gift of Food

Sharing food is a deeply spiritual act that fosters connection and community. When we offer food to others, we provide physical nourishment and share a part of ourselves. Serve meals with mindfulness and care. Create a beautiful presentation, set a welcoming table, and invite others to share the meal with you. Encourage a moment of silence or a shared blessing before eating, acknowledging the effort and love that went into the preparation.

1. Before starting the meal, invite everyone to gather around the table.

2. Take a moment to sit down to appreciate the food and the company.

3. Offer a simple blessing, such as: "May this food nourish our bodies, may this time nourish our spirits, and may our hearts be filled with gratitude and love."

Foraging Basics

Foraging for wild food is a practice that reconnects us with the natural world, enhancing our awareness of the seasons and the bounty they bring. It has become a popular pastime recently, a reflection of our growing interest in ancient practices. It is a reminder that our kitchens are extensions of the natural environment, where the earth's gifts are transformed into nourishing meals. Foraging can be a simple and enriching way to incorporate wild, seasonal ingredients into your cooking, fostering a deeper connection to the land and its rhythms.

Foraging inherently ties us to the cycles of nature, as different plants and herbs become available at various times of the year. This awareness of seasonality encourages us to adapt our cooking practices to what is naturally abundant, promoting a diverse and harmonious diet in harmony with the earth's rhythms. Examples of seasonal foraging:

- Look for young greens like dandelion leaves and wild garlic, which can be added to salads and soups.

- Berries such as blackberries and raspberries are plentiful and can be used in desserts and preserves.

- Mushrooms and nuts are abundant and can be included in hearty stews and baking.

Unprocessed Food and Thinking

Including foraged foods in your kitchen rituals helps shift your mindset toward unprocessed, natural ingredients. This approach reduces the reliance on heavily processed foods that often contain additives and preservatives, which can contribute to toxicity in the body, mind, and home. Enroll in a local foraging course, explore your locality, and learn about the seasonal gifts it will share

- Equip yourself with a foraging basket or bag, a guidebook to local edible plants, and perhaps a pair of scissors or a knife.

- Spend time in nature, observing the plants and their growth patterns. Note the environment and its health, as this affects the quality of the plants you forage.

- Only take what you need, leaving plenty for wildlife and ensuring the plants can thrive. Harvest mindfully, with gratitude for the earth's bounty.

- Bring your foraged finds home and integrate them into your meals. For example, fresh, wild herbs can enhance the flavor of your dish and provide unique nutritional benefits.

Less Toxicity in Body, Mind, and Home

Processed foods often carry chemical additives, pesticides, and other harmful substances that can accumulate in our systems, leading to various health issues. To detoxify meal preparation:

1. Focus on fresh, whole foods that you can find in nature from local farmers' markets.

2. Use simple cooking methods, such as streaming, roasting, or raw preparation, to preserve the natural nutrients of the ingredients.

3. Practice mindful eating, paying attention to the flavors, textures, and nourishment that each bite provides. This promotes a deeper connection to your food and a more satisfying eating experience.

This shift toward unprocessed, natural foods reduces toxicity in our bodies, minds, and homes, promoting overall well-being.

Origins and Significance of Ingredients

For the modern witch, understanding the origins and significance of ingredients is crucial to creating magical and nourishing meals. Ingredients are not merely components of a recipe; they carry the energy of the places they come from and the hands that harvested them.

In today's world, the modern witch has the convenience of supermarkets and natural hedgerows, blending the best of both realms to create a well-rounded, magical kitchen.

- **Supermarkets:** While supermarkets offer a wide variety of ingredients year-round, it is important to choose items that align with your values and needs when possible, especially for organic and sustainably sourced products. Reading labels and understanding certifications can help you make informed choices that support your health and the environment.

- **Hedgerows and foraging:** Foraging is a way to connect directly with the earth and the natural cycles of growth and harvest. Hedgerows, forests, and fields offer a bounty of wild edibles that change with the seasons. This practice provides fresh, nutrient-rich ingredients and deepens your connection to nature and its rhythms.

- **Farmers' markets:** One of the best ways to become seasonally aware is to seek out your local farmers' market. Farmers' markets offer fresh, locally grown produce that is often harvested at its peak. Engaging with local farmers allows you to learn about the seasonal cycles of your region and the best times to enjoy certain fruits and vegetables.

Ingredients Place in Your Life

Understanding the place of ingredients in your life involves recognizing their nutritional, energetic, and symbolic roles. Each ingredient brings its own properties and benefits, contributing to the overall energy of the meal.

- **Nutritional value:** Fresh, seasonal ingredients are packed with nutrients that nourish your body. Eating seasonally ensures you get the freshest and most nutrient-dense food available.

- **Energetic properties:** Each ingredient carries specific energetic properties that can enhance your magical workings.

For example, basil is known for its protective qualities, while rosemary is often used for purification and memory.

- **Symbolic significance:** Many ingredients have symbolic meanings in different cultures and traditions. Apples, for instance, are often associated with love and wisdom, while grains like wheat symbolize abundance and prosperity.

- **Ingredients with Intention**

    o Spend a morning at your local farmers market. Engage with the vendors, ask about their growing practices, and choose ingredients that resonate with you.

    o Take a walk in nature and forage for wild herbs, berries, or mushrooms. Make sure to identify plants correctly and harvest sustainably.

    o When shopping at a supermarket, take the time to read labels and choose organic or locally sourced products. Imagine the journey of each ingredient and the energy it brings to your kitchen.

Cooking Mindfully and Slowly

Cooking mindfully and slowly is a sacred act, transforming the mundane into the magical. In our fast-paced world, it's easy to rush through meal preparation, but true kitchen craft invites us to slow down, be present, and infuse each step with intention and energy.

Begin your cooking ritual by lighting a candle. The gentle flame serves as a reminder to slow down and focus on the task. Its warm, flickering light creates a serene atmosphere, allowing you to center yourself and connect deeply with cooking. Take a moment to breathe deeply and set your intention for the meal.

As you gather your ingredients, handle each one with care and gratitude. Acknowledge the journey each ingredient has taken to reach your kitchen and the energy it holds. Feel the textures, inhale the aromas, and appreciate the colors. This mindful appreciation opens your senses and deepens your connection to the food. Imagine the energy flowing from your hands into the ingredients, infusing them with positive intentions.

When you begin to cook, move with grace and purpose. Chop vegetables slowly, savoring the rhythm of the knife against the cutting board. Stir pots deliberately, imagining each circle as a spiral of energy, drawing your intentions into the food. As you measure spices, remember that each one carries its own magical properties. Sprinkle them thoughtfully, visualizing their energies blending harmoniously to enhance the meal's potency.

Cleaning up is just as important as the cooking process. Approach it with the same mindfulness and care. As you wash dishes, imagine the water cleansing away physical residue and any lingering negative energy.

Let the candle's flame keep you grounded and focused throughout the process. Its light reminds you to stay present, making each step meditative. If your mind starts to wander, gently bring it back to the candle's glow and the rhythm of your movements. This mindfulness practice transforms cooking from a chore into a sacred ritual, filled with power and intention.

The Importance of Emotional State in Cooking

The energy and emotions you bring into your kitchen play a crucial role in the quality and nourishment of the food you prepare. Cooking when you are upset or angry can infuse your meals with negative vibrations, which can affect the well-being of those who consume it. Food is not just physical sustenance; it is a vessel for the energy and intentions of the cook. Therefore, maintaining a positive and calm emotional state is essential for creating nourishing and uplifting meals.

When you find yourself feeling upset or angry, it is wise to take a moment to center yourself before stepping into the kitchen. Light a candle and take a few deep breaths to ground yourself. Lighting a candle serves as a simple yet powerful ritual that can shift your focus and bring you into a state of mindfulness. Its steady flame represents clarity and calm, helping to dispel negative emotions and create a serene atmosphere.

If your emotions are particularly intense, consider performing a quick meditation or grounding exercise before you begin cooking. Close your eyes, visualize roots growing from your feet into the earth, and feel the stability and strength of the ground beneath you. This connection to the earth can help balance your energy and bring you back to a calm place.

The Power of Positive Energy in Food

As you prepare your ingredients, be mindful of the energy you transmit. Positive emotions such as love, gratitude, and joy can elevate the vibrational frequency of your food, making it more nourishing and healing. Visualize your positive energy flowing from your hands into the ingredients, infusing them with love and light. This practice enhances the food's flavor and nutritional value and creates a meal that uplifts and supports those who eat it.

When your emotional state is aligned with your intentions, cooking becomes a form of alchemy, transforming raw ingredients into a meal that nourishes the body and soul. This mindful approach to cooking ensures that every dish you prepare reflects your highest self, filled with positive energy and intention.

Sitting down to eat is a sacred act that honors the food you have prepared and the people you share it with. It is a moment to express gratitude for the earth's nourishment and to acknowledge the effort that went into preparing the meal. This practice of mindful eating fosters a deeper connection to food and enhances the dining experience.

Candlelight is a wonderful way to bring focus and intention to the dining table. The soft, flickering light creates a warm, inviting atmosphere, encouraging relaxation and conversation. It helps to center your attention on the present moment, making eating a meditative experience.

The ritual of eating mindfully is easy. When you eat, take a moment to appreciate the food before you. Allow yourself to fully experience the colors, aromas, and textures of the meal. Begin your meal with silence or a simple blessing, expressing gratitude for the food and the hand that prepared it. This gratitude ritual sets a positive tone and enhances the meal's energy.

Creating a Sacred Dining Space

To further honor the food and those you are with, create a sacred dining space that reflects your intentions. Set the table carefully, using dishes and utensils with special meaning or beauty. Add elements such as fresh flowers, crystals, or a beautiful tablecloth to enhance the aesthetic and energetic qualities of the space.

Encourage open and positive conversation at the table, fostering community and connection. Share stories, express gratitude, and listen attentively to one another. This mindful communication practice strengthens the bonds between you and your fellow diners and enhances the overall dining experience.

Cooking Spell to Bless Your Abundance in the Kitchen

Creating a spell to bless your abundance in the kitchen can enhance the purpose and flavors of your food and fill meals with love and positive energy.

Materials needed

- a green candle (symbolizing abundance and prosperity)
- a pink candle (symbolizing love and harmony)

- a small dish of sea salt (for purification)
- a small dish of sugar (for sweetness and joy)
- fresh herbs (such as basil for prosperity, rosemary for protection, and thyme for courage)
- a wooden spoon (to stir your intentions into your cooking)

Steps

1. Clean and tidy your kitchen to create a welcoming and sacred environment. Light some incense or diffuse essential oils to clear any negative energy and set a positive atmosphere.

2. Place the green and pink candles in a central location in your kitchen. Light the green candle first, focusing on the intention of abundance and prosperity filling your kitchen. Then, light the pink candle, focusing on the intention of love and harmony infusing your space.

3. Sprinkle a small circle of sea salt on your workspace. Inside this circle, sprinkle a smaller circle of sugar. This represents the purification and sweetness you are inviting into your kitchen.

4. Place the fresh herbs inside the circle of salt and sugar. As you do, visualize their properties (prosperity, protection, and courage) being activated and spreading throughout your kitchen.

5. Take the wooden spoon and hold it over the candles, allowing the flames to symbolize the activation of your spell. Then, stir the air inside the circle three times clockwise, saying: "By earth, by air, by fire, by sea, abundance and flavor, come to me. With love and joy in every bite, bless this kitchen day and night."

6. Touch the wooden spoon to your cooking tools, such as pots, pans, and utensils, visualizing them filled with the same energy of abundance, flavor, and love.

7. Once you feel the energy has been sufficiently infused, extinguish the candles, giving thanks for their help in your spell. Leave the salt, sugar, and herbs in place for a few hours or overnight to fully absorb the energies before discarding them outside to return to the earth.

8. Whenever you cook, remember to stir your food clockwise to invite positive energy and counterclockwise to banish negativity. As you cook, focus on your intentions of abundance, flavor, and love, knowing that each dish you prepare is blessed with these energies.

As we have journeyed through the sacred art of kitchen craft, we have explored the profound impact of our emotional state, intentions, and mindful practices on the food we prepare and share. By cooking with love, gratitude, and awareness, and by creating a sacred dining space that honors both the food and the people gathered, we transform every meal into a nourishing ritual that uplifts and connects us to gratitude, each other, and the gift and power of food.

Chapter 7:

Magical Food Recipes for Spiritual and Physical Nourishment and Health

This is where the enchantment of kitchen craft reaches its peak with a collection of magical food recipes designed to nourish both the body and spirit. In this chapter, you will discover how to transform everyday ingredients into powerful spiritual and physical well-being sources. I have chosen to illustrate the Old ways of food preparation with a single recipe for each method, Baking, Stewing, Broths and Soups, and finally Roasting. This is just the start of your culinary adventures! Each recipe is crafted with intention, combining the wisdom of ancient culinary traditions with the magic of modern witchcraft. Whether you are seeking healing, vitality, or a deeper connection to the divine, these recipes will guide you in creating meals that are as spiritually enriching as they are delicious.

Seasonality and Its Use

Seasonal eating connects you to the natural world in a profound way. When you consume foods that are in season, you are eating them at their freshest and most nutritious. Seasonal produce is often richer in vitamins and minerals because it is harvested at its peak ripeness. This natural abundance of nutrients supports your physical health, providing your body with the essential elements it needs to thrive.

Furthermore, seasonal foods carry the energetic imprint of the time of year they are grown. For example, spring greens like dandelion and nettle are perfect for detoxification after a long winter, while autumnal foods like pumpkins and squash are grounding and nourishing, preparing you for the colder months ahead.

Harnessing Seasonal Energy in Your Cooking

Including seasonal ingredients in your recipes can significantly enhance their magical properties. Each season brings a unique energy and set of intentions that you can harness in your cooking.

- **Spring:** This season is all about renewal and growth. Fresh greens, herbs, and young vegetables are abundant, symbolizing new beginnings and cleansing. Include ingredients like asparagus, radishes, and mint into your dishes to welcome the revitalizing energy of spring.

- **Summer:** Summer is a time of abundance and vitality. The long days and warm weather produce a plethora of fruits and vegetables. Ingredients like tomatoes, cucumbers, berries, and basil bring the sun's vibrant energy into your meals, supporting joy, creativity, and expansion.

- **Autumn:** The harvest season is a time for grounding and preparation. Root vegetables, squashes, and hearty greens are in abundance. Foods like pumpkins, sweet potatoes, and kale provide grounding energy, helping you center and nourish yourself as you prepare for winter.

- **Winter:** Winter is a time for introspection and rest. The earth's energy retreats inward and so should our diets. Include warming, nourishing foods like root vegetables, hearty grains, and warming spices like cinnamon and nutmeg. These ingredients support your body and spirit during the colder, darker months.

Practical Tips for Eating Seasonally

1. **Grow your own.** If possible, grow your herbs and vegetables. This ensures you have access to fresh, seasonal ingredients and allows you to infuse your food with your energy and intentions from seed to harvest.

2. **Plan your meals.** Plan your meals around seasonal availability. This supports your health and reduces your environmental footprint, as seasonal foods require less transportation and storage.

3. **Preserve the harvest.** Learn techniques for preserving seasonal abundance, such as canning, freezing, and drying. This allows you to enjoy the benefits of seasonal eating throughout the year.

The Magic of Breadmaking

Breadmaking is one of the oldest and most revered culinary traditions, rich with symbolic and magical significance. In many cultures, bread is considered a sacred food, representing sustenance, abundance, and life cycle.

Bread is deeply symbolic in witchcraft, often associated with the earth element due to its foundational ingredients of grain and water. Baking bread can be seen as an alchemical transformation, where simple ingredients are combined and transformed through the magic of fermentation and the heat of the oven. This mirrors many spiritual practices where transformation and creation are central themes.

Kneading dough is a meditative act that connects you to the ancient rhythms of life and the cycles of nature. As you knead, you infuse the dough with your energy and intentions. The rising of the dough symbolizes growth and expansion, while the baking process represents transformation and manifestation. Sharing bread with others is an act of community and connection, spreading the blessings and intentions imbued in the loaf.

Simple Herb-Infused Bread (Tiffany, 2022)

This herb-infused bread is perfect for rituals and gatherings, bringing the magic of fresh herbs into your baking. The combination of rosemary and thyme adds flavor and infuses the bread with protection and courage.

Prep time: 20 minutes

Cook time: 25–30 minutes

Total time: 1 hour, 50 minutes (including rising time)

Nutrition	Serving size	Protein	Carbs	Calories	Protein
Per serving	2 slices	4 g	26 g	150	4 g

Ingredients

- 3 cup all-purpose flour
- 1 tbsp sugar
- 1 tbsp salt
- 1 packet (2 1/4 tsp) active dry yeast
- 1 cup warm water (110 °F to 115 °F)
- 2 tbsp olive oil
- 2 tbsp chopped fresh rosemary

- 1 tbsp chopped fresh thyme

Instructions

1. Combine the flour, sugar, and salt in a large bowl. In a separate bowl, dissolve the yeast in the warm water. Let it sit for about five minutes until it becomes frothy. Add the yeast mixture and olive oil to the dry ingredients. Mix until a dough forms.

2. Transfer the dough to a floured surface and knead for about 10 minutes until it becomes smooth and elastic. As you knead, focus on your intentions for the bread, infusing it with thoughts of protection and courage. Visualize the energy of the rosemary and thyme, enhancing these properties.

3. Place the dough in a lightly oiled bowl, cover it with a damp cloth, and let it rise in a warm place for about one hour, or until it has doubled.

4. Punch down the dough and transfer it to a floured surface. Shape it into a loaf and place it on a greased pan or a baking sheet.

5. Cover the dough with a damp cloth and let it rise for another 30 minutes.

6. Preheat your oven to 375 °F (190 °C). Bake the bread for 25-30 minutes or until it sounds hollow when tapped on the bottom. The crust should be golden brown.

7. Allow the bread to cool on a wire rack. Before serving, hold the loaf in your hands and say a blessing or affirmation, infusing it with love and positive energy.

The History of Stews and Broths

Stews and broths are some of the oldest forms of cooking, dating back to ancient times when humans first began to use fire and primitive cooking vessels. These hearty dishes were essential for survival, making the most of available resources and creating nourishing meals from simple ingredients. With its combination of meat, vegetables, and herbs, stew provided a complete and filling meal. In contrast, broths, made of simmering bones and vegetables, served as a refreshing and healing drink.

Magical Hearty Harvest Stew (Megan, 2021)

This stew is perfect for grounding and nourishment, especially in autumn.

Prep time: 20 minutes

Cook time: 1 hour, 30 minutes

Total time: 1 hour, 50 minutes

Nutrition	Number of servings	Calories	Protein	Fat	Carbs
Per serving	5	250	10 g	7 g	35 g

Ingredients

- 1 lb beef stew meat, cubed
- 2 tbsp olive oil
- 1 large onion, chopped

- 3 cloves garlic, minced
- 3 carrots, chopped
- 3 potatoes, chopped
- 2 parsnips, chopped
- 1 cup butternut squash, cubed
- 1 cup green beans, chopped
- 4 cup red wine (optional)
- 2 tbsp tomato paste
- 1 tsp dried thyme
- 1 tsp dried rosemary
- Salt and pepper to taste
- Fresh parsley, chopped (for garnish)

Instructions

1. Gather and chop all vegetables, ensuring they are cut into similar sizes for even cooking.
2. Heat the olive oil over medium-high heat in a large pot. Add the beef cubes and brown on all sides for about five to seven minutes. Remove the beef and set it aside.
3. Add the onion and garlic to the same pot and saute until fragrant and translucent, about five minutes.
4. Return the beef to the pot. Add the carrots, potatoes, parsnips, butternut squash, and green beans. Pour in the beef broth and red wine, if using. Stir in the tomato paste, thyme, and rosemary.

5. Bring the mixture to a boil, then reduce the heat to low. Cover and simmer for one hour, stirring occasionally, until the vegetables are tender and the flavors have melted together.

6. Season with salt and pepper to taste. Serve hot, garnish with fresh parsley. As you serve, focus on grounding and nourishing intentions, visualizing the stew, and providing warmth and substance.

Healing Herbal Broth (Natasha, 2020)

Perfect for illness or fatigue, it combines the nourishing qualities of chicken bones with the healing properties of herbs. Sip it slowly, allowing warmth and energy to soothe your body and spirit.

Prep time: 15 minutes

Cook time: 4–6 hours

Nutrition	Serving size	Calories	Protein	Fat	Carbs
Per serving	1 cup	70	7 g	3 g	4 g

Ingredients

- 2 lb of chicken bones (with some meat)
- 1 large onion, quartered
- 3 cloves garlic, smashed
- 3 carrots, chopped
- 3 celery stalks, chopped
- 1 bay leaf

- 1 tsp dried thyme
- 1 tsp dried rosemary
- 1 tsp dried sage
- 1 tbsp apple cider vinegar
- 10 cup water
- salt and pepper to taste
- fresh parsley, chopped (for garnish)

Instructions

1. Gather all the ingredients. Roughly chop the vegetables; there is no need to peel them, as they will be strained out later.
2. In a large stockpot, combine the ingredients, including the water.
3. Bring the mixture to a boil over high heat. Once boiling, reduce the heat to low and let it simmer gently.
4. Allow the broth to simmer for four to six hours, skimming off any foam that rises to the top. The longer it simmers, the more nutrients and flavor will be extracted from the bones and vegetables.
5. After simmering, strain the broth through a fine-mesh sieve into a large bowl, discarding the solids; season with salt and pepper to taste.
6. Serve the broth hot, garnished with fresh parsley. Store any leftovers in the refrigerator for up to five days or freeze for up to three months. As you sip the broth, visualize its healing energy, restoring your body and mind.

The History of Roasts

Roasting meat over an open flame is one of the oldest cooking methods. It enhances the flavor and texture of meat while preserving its nutrients. In ancient times, roasting was a practical cooking method with significant ceremonial and communal value. Large gatherings and feasts often featured roasted meats, which symbolized abundance, prosperity, and the communal sharing of sustenance.

In the context of witchcraft, roasts carry deep symbolic meanings. The act of roasting meat, often in the heart of the home, the hearth, aligns with the element energies of fire and earth. Fire transforms the raw ingredients, symbolizing purification and change, while the earth sustains the eater. Preparing a roast can be a sacred ritual, imbuing the meal with magical intentions such as protection, abundance, and familial harmony.

Magical Herb-Encrusted Roast Beef (Herb-Crusted Roast Beef, 2023)

This dish nourishes the body and fills your home with warm, savory aromas that enhance the spirit of abundance and togetherness.

Prep time: 15 minutes

Cook time: 1 hour, 30 minutes

Nutrient	Number of servings	Calories	Protein	Carbs	Fat
Per serving	12	320	28 g	3 g	20 g

Ingredients

- 3 lb beef roast (such as ribeye or sirloin)
- 2 tbsp olive oil
- 4 cloves garlic, minced
- 2 tbsp fresh rosemary, chopped
- 1 tbsp fresh thyme, chopped
- 1 tbsp fresh oregano, chopped
- 1 tsp salt
- 1 tsp black pepper

Instruction

1. Preheat your oven to 375 °F (190 °C). Pat the beef roast dry with paper towels. This helps the herbs and oil adhere better.//
2. In a small bowl, combine the olive oil, minced garlic, rosemary, thyme, oregano, salt, and pepper. Mix well to form a paste.
3. Rub the herb mixture all over the beef roast, ensuring it is evenly coated. As you do this, focus on your intentions of protection and abundance, infusing the meat with these energies.
4. Place the roast on a rack in a roasting pan. Roast in the preheated oven for about 1 hour and 30 minutes, or until the internal temperature reaches your desired level of doneness (130 °F for medium-rare, 140 °F for medium).
5. Remove the roast from the oven and let it rest for 15 minutes before carving. This redistributes the juices, ensuring a tender and flavorful roast.

6. Carve the roast and serve it on a platter. Before eating, hold hands over the meat and say a blessing or affirmation, visualizing the meal as providing protection and abundance to all who partake.

The History of Vegetables in Cooking

Cultivated from the earliest days of farming, vegetables have provided essential vitamins, minerals, and fiber necessary for health and well-being. They have also held significant cultural and symbolic meanings in various societies, often associated with fertility, abundance, and renewal.

In witchcraft, vegetables are revered for their natural energies and magical properties. Each vegetable carries its own unique vibrational frequency and symbolism, which can be harnessed for various spells and rituals. Root vegetables, for example, are grounding and protective, while leafy greens are often used for purification and prosperity. Cooking with vegetables is a way to connect with the earth's bounty and infuse your meals with the energies of growth, healing, and transformation.

Magical Roasted Root Vegetables (Elkus, 2023)

This recipe combines the earth's robust and hearty offerings, making it ideal for a comforting meal that connects you to the foundational energies of nature.

Prep time: 15 minutes

Cook time: 40 minutes

Nutrient	Number of servings	Calories	Protein	Fat	Carbs
Per serving	5	200	3 g	10 g	28 g

Ingredients

- 2 large carrots, chopped
- 2 parsnips, chopped
- 2 sweet potatoes, cubed
- 1 large beet, cubed
- 1 red onion, quartered
- 3 cloves garlic, minced
- 3 tbsp olive oil
- 1 tbsp fresh rosemary, chopped
- 1 tbsp fresh thyme, chopped
- salt and pepper to taste

Instructions

1. Preheat your oven to 425 °F (220 °C). Wash and chop all the vegetables into even-sized pieces to ensure they cook evenly.
2. Combine the chopped vegetables, minced garlic, olive oil, rosemary, and thyme in a large bowl. Toss well to coat. As you mix, focus on your intentions of grounding and protection, visualizing the energies the vegetables absorb.

3. Spread the vegetables in a single layer on a baking sheet. Season with salt and pepper. Roast in the oven for about 40 minutes, or until the vegetables are tender and golden brown, stirring halfway through.

4. Transfer the roasted vegetables to a serving dish. Before eating, hold your hands over the dish and say a blessing or affirmation, visualizing the meal as providing grounding and protective energies.

The History of Fungi in Cooking

Fungi, or mushrooms, have a long and storied history in culinary traditions and magical practices. Revered for their unique flavors and powerful health benefits, mushrooms have been used for thousands of years in various cultures. Ancient Egyptians considered mushrooms food and royalty, while in China, certain mushrooms like reishi and shiitake were used in traditional medicine for their healing properties.

Mushrooms grow in dark, moist environments and symbolize mystery, transformation, and the unseen. They are associated with the element of earth and are believed to carry potent energies for protection, healing, and spiritual growth. Cooking with mushrooms can be a deeply mystical experience, allowing you to tap into their ancient wisdom and harness their magical properties.

Magical Creamy Mushroom Soup (Karina, 2018)

Combining the rich flavors of various mushrooms with a creamy base, this soup offers physical sustenance and spiritual renewal.

Prep time: 15 minutes

Cook time: 30 minutes

Nutrients	Number of servings	Calories	Protein	Fat	Carbs
Per serving	6	200	6 g	15 g	14 g

Ingredients

- 1 lb mixed mushrooms (cremini, shiitake, and portobello), sliced
- 1 medium onion, chopped
- 3 cloves garlic, minced
- 2 tbsp olive oil
- 4 cup vegetable broth
- 1 cup heavy cream
- 1 tbsp fresh thyme, chopped
- 1 tbsp fresh parsley, chopped
- salt and pepper to taste

Instructions

1. Wash and slice the mushrooms. Chop the onions and mince the garlic.
2. Heat the olive oil over medium heat in a large pot. Add the onion and garlic, and saute until fragrant and translucent, about five minutes. Add the mushrooms and cook until they release their juice and become tender, about ten minutes.

3. Pour in the vegetable broth and bring to a boil. Reduce the heat and let it simmer for 15 minutes to allow the flavors to meld together.

4. Use an immersion blender to blend the soup until smooth. Alternatively, you can carefully transfer the soup to a blender and blend it in batches. Return the blended soup to the pot and stir in the heavy cream.

5. Stir in the fresh thyme and parsley. Season with salt and pepper to taste. Serve hot, garnished with additional fresh herbs. As you serve, visualize the soup providing grounding and healing energy to all who partake.

Herbs for Cooking

Herbs have been used in cooking for centuries to enhance food flavor and imbue meals with their natural properties and energies. Herbs are both foods and medicines. Each herb has a unique flavor profile and aromatic qualities, transforming ordinary dishes into extraordinary culinary experiences. A few of the most popular are listed below.

Basil, often called the "king of herbs," adds a fresh, slightly sweet flavor to dishes and is commonly used in Mediterranean and Italian cuisines. Its vibrant green leaves provide a visual delight and carry properties of love and protection.

Oregano, another robust herb, brings a warm, peppery flavor to Italian and Greek dishes. Its leaves are rich in antioxidants and are used in spells for happiness and tranquility. Parsley, often seen as a simple garnish, adds a fresh, slightly peppery taste to food and is used in magic for purification and protection.

Sage is a powerful herb both in the kitchen and in magical practices. Known for its earthy, slightly peppery flavor, it enhances the taste of meats, particularly poultry, and can add depth to vegetable dishes and soups. Beyond its culinary uses, sage has long been revered for its protective qualities. Including sage in your cooking enriches your meals and invites protective and purifying energy into your home, aligning your culinary creations with the sacred practice of hearth magic.

Rosemary, with its robust, pine-like flavor, is a versatile herb that pairs well with a variety of dishes, from roasted meats and potatoes to savory breads and stews. This aromatic herb is also a powerful tool in witchcraft, symbolizing remembrance, clarity, and fidelity. Its magical properties are often used to enhance memory and concentration, making it a valuable addition to rituals and spells focused on mental clarity and protection. Including rosemary in your cooking elevates your culinary creations. It also weaves the energies of remembrance and protection into your daily life, creating a bridge between the mundane and the mystical.

Thyme is a fragrant herb with a subtle, slightly minty flavor that enhances the taste of soups, stews, and roasted vegetables. In the realm of witchcraft, thyme is celebrated for its purifying and healing properties and is often used in spells and rituals to attract good health, courage, and protection. Adding thyme to your cooking can do more than just flavor your dishes; it can also infuse your meals with energy and vitality. By integrating thyme into your kitchen magic, you create nourishing meals that satisfy the body and uplift the spirit, promoting overall well-being and resilience.

Chamomile, with its gentle and sweet flavor, is renowned for its anti-inflammatory and calming effects. Chamomile tea is a popular remedy for digestive issues, insomnia, and anxiety, providing a natural way to soothe the mind and body. Peppermint, another versatile herb, relieves digestive problems such as bloating, gas, and indigestion. Its refreshing aroma can also help to alleviate headaches and improve mental focus.

As we have explored the enchanting world of culinary and medicinal herbs, we have uncovered the profound ways these natural wonders enhance our lives, both in the kitchen and in our well-being.

Now, with a deeper understanding of herbs' powerful role in our daily rituals and health practices, it is time to look at the broader picture of maintaining balance in our homes throughout the year. In the next chapter, we will explore how to align our living spaces and practices with the natural cycles of the seasons. By tuning to the rhythms of nature, we can create a harmonious environment that supports our spiritual and physical well-being year-round.

Chapter 8:

Maintaining the Balance of Hearth and Home

When we become aware of the home we have in nature, we sense home in whatever place we're in. –Casper Ter Kuile

No matter the locality of our homes, we live in nature and with the rhythms of the season. Our homes are not isolated havens—they are intrinsically connected to the natural world outside. By recognizing and honoring these connections, we can create a harmonious flow of energy between our living spaces and the broader landscape, ensuring that our homes remain vibrant and balanced all year.

Get to Know Your Corner of the Universe

Getting to know your corner of the universe is important for truly maintaining the balance of your heart and home throughout the seasonal year. This means developing a deep awareness of the natural world surrounding your home and understanding how its rhythms and energies influence your life. Every place on Earth has its own unique spirit and energy, shaped by geography, climate, flora, and fauna.

Start by observing the natural landscape around you. Spend time in your garden, local parks, forests, and beaches. Notice the types of plants that thrive in your area and the weather patterns that shape the environment. Each element carries its own magical properties and can be a source of inspiration and power for your rituals and spells. For example, if you live near the ocean, you might incorporate sea salt and shells into your practices, drawing on the ocean's cleansing and transformative energies.

Bringing the outside in is a powerful way to maintain the balance of your home. Decorate your living space with natural elements that reflect the current season. In spring, you might fill your home with fresh flowers and new growth and renewal-budding branches. In summer, include vibrant, sunlit colors and symbols of abundance. Autumn might bring warm, earthy tones and harvest decorations, while winter could see the introduction of evergreen boughs and candles to represent light in the darkness.

Wheel of Seasons, Weathers, Stars, and Moon Energy

The wheel of the year is a fundamental concept in many nature-based spiritual traditions, including modern witchcraft and paganism. It represents the cyclical nature of the seasons and the continuous flow of time, guiding practitioners through the natural world's rhythms. Each sabbat holds its own unique energy and symbolism, reflecting the natural changes occurring around us.

- **Yule (winter solstice):** Celebrated around December 21st, Yule marks the longest night of the year and the sun's rebirth. It's a time for introspection, rest, and renewal. The cold and stillness of winter encourage us to turn inward, reflect on the past year, and set intentions for the future.

- **Imbolc:** Celebrated around February 1st, Imbolc heralds the first signs of spring. It is a time of purification and preparation, symbolized by the emerging light and the earliest buds of new growth.

- **Ostara (spring equinox):** Around March 21st, Ostara celebrates the balance of day and night and the full arrival of spring. This festival honors fertility, rebirth, and new beginnings, with nature bursting into life.

- **Beltane:** Celebrated around May 1st, Beltane is a fire festival marking the peak of spring and the approaching summer. It is a time of passion, fertility, and vibrant energy.

- **Litha (summer solstice):** Around June 21st, Litha celebrates the longest day of the year and the sun's power at its zenith. It is a time of abundance, strength, and joy.

- **Lammas (Lughnasadh):** Celebrated around August 1st, this festival marks the beginning of the harvest season. It is a time of gratitude and reflection on the fruits of our labor.

- **Mabon (autumn equinox):** Around September 21st, Mabon celebrates the balance of day and night and the second harvest. It is a time of thanksgiving and preparing for the coming winter.

- **Samhain:** Celebrated around October 31st, Samhain marks the end of the harvest and the beginning of winter. It is a time to honor ancestors, reflect on mortality, and embrace the cycle of life and death.

Stars and Moon Energy

In addition to the seasons, the stars and moon play a crucial role in shaping the energies we work with in witchcraft. The moon's phases, in particular, are deeply influential, each offering its own unique energy for magical work.

- **New moon:** A time for new beginnings and setting intentions. The darkness of the new moon represents a clean slate, perfect for planting seeds of future goals and dreams.

- **Waxing moon:** As the moon grows in light, it is a time for growth, expansion, and taking action. This phase is ideal for increasing attraction and building spells.

- **Full moon:** The full moon is a time of peak energy and power. It is perfect for manifestation, completion, and celebrating achievements. Rituals performed during the full moon are potent and highly charged.

- **Waning moon:** As the moon decreases in light, it is a time for release, reflection, and banishing. This phase is suitable for letting go of what no longer serves you and clearing space for new growth.

- **Dark moon:** The final phase before the new moon, a time of rest and introspection. It is ideal for deep reflection, shadow work, and connecting with inner wisdom.

Connecting With the Stars

Astrology also plays a significant role in witchcraft, with the planets' positions influencing our energy and actions. Each zodiac sign carries its own unique traits and energies, and the sun's journey through these signs affects us differently. For instance, when the sun is in Aries, it brings a surge of energy and drive, making it an excellent time for initiating new projects. Conversely, the sun in Taurus encourages stability, patience, and enjoying the fruits of our labor.

Here are some ways to integrate these energies into your practice:

- **Seasonal altars:** Decorate your altar with symbols and elements representing the current season. This helps you stay attuned to the natural cycles and infuses your space with the energy of the sabbat.

- **Lunar rituals:** Plan your rituals according to the moon phases. Set intentions during the new moon, perform growth spells during the waxing moon, celebrate manifestations during the full moon, and release during the waning moon.

- **Astrological insights:** Pay attention to the astrological calendar and include the energies of the zodiac signs in your practices. Use the qualities of each sign to guide your spell work and intentions.

Purposeful Seasonal Rituals and Actions

Embracing the earth's natural rhythms through purposeful seasonal rituals and actions allows you to create a deeper connection with the world around you. These rituals honor the changing energies of the seasons and help you align your personal and spiritual growth with the cycles of nature.

Planting Seeds of Intention: A Spring Ritual

Spring is when the earth awakens from its slumber, and life begins to blossom again. This energy is perfect for setting new intentions and planting the seeds of future endeavors.

Materials needed

- small pots or a garden plot
- seeds (herbs, flowers, or vegetables)
- potting soil
- a small trowel
- a piece of paper and a pen
- a green candle (symbolizing growth and renewal)

Steps

1. Find a quiet and comfortable place in your garden or home. Light the green candle to signify the energy of growth and new beginnings.

2. On the piece of paper, write down your intentions or goals for the coming season. Be specific and focus on the positive outcomes you wish to manifest.

3. Fill the pots with soil using the trowel. As you plant each seed, hold your written intentions in your mind, visualizing them growing and flourishing just like the seeds you are planting.

4. Gently water the seeds, imagining the water as a source of nourishment for your intention. Place the pots in a sunny spot where they can receive plenty of light.

5. Recite an affirmation or blessing to seal your intentions. For example: "As these seeds grow and bloom, so will my intentions. May they flourish with the energy of spring, bringing new beginnings and abundant blessings."

6. Extinguish the candle and take a moment to feel the energy of the earth and the potential for growth within you.

Celebrating Abundance and Vitality in the Summer: A Ritual

A purposeful summer ritual might involve creating a gratitude altar or holding a feast to honor the abundance in your life.

Material needed

- a small table or flat surface
- fresh flowers
- seasonal fruits and vegetables
- candles (yellow or gold, symbolizing the sun)
- items that represent abundance to you (coins, crystals, etc.)

Steps

1. Find a place in your home or garden to set up your gratitude altar. Arrange the table or surface with the items you have gathered.

2. Place fresh flowers on the altar to represent the beauty and abundance of summer. Arrange them in a way that feels pleasing to you.

3. Display seasonal fruits and vegetables on the altar. These represent the harvest and the rewards of your hard work.

4. Light the yellow or gold candles to symbolize the sun's energy and the vibrant life force of summer.

5. Take a moment to reflect on the abundance in your life. Speak out loud or silently express your gratitude for the blessings you have received. You might say: "I am grateful for the abundance that fills my life. May the energy of summer bring joy, vitality, and continued blessings."

6. You can choose to hold a small feast with friends or family, sharing the fruits and vegetables from your altar as a way to celebrate and give thanks.

Harvesting and Reflection: An Autumn Ritual

The energy of this season encourages us to gather the fruits of our labor, give thanks, and reflect on the past year.

Materials needed

- a wreath base (grapevine, straw, or wire)
- autumn leaves, acorns, pine cones, and dried flowers
- ribbon (orange, brown, or gold)

- hot glue gun or floral wire
- scissors

Steps

1. Gather all your materials and find a comfortable place to work. Take a moment to center yourself and set your intention for the ritual.

2. Start by attaching the leaves, acorns, pine cones, and dried flowers to the wreath base using a hot glue gun or floral wire. As you work, reflect on the accomplishments and blessings you have received this year.

3. Tie a ribbon around the wreath, creating a bow or weaving it through the wreath. The colors of the ribbon should represent the warmth and richness of the autumn season.

4. Think about what you have harvested regarding personal growth, achievements, and lessons learned. You might say: "As I create this wreath, I honor the harvest of my efforts and the blessings of the past year. May this season of reflection and gratitude guide me into the future."

5. Hang the wreath on your door or in your home as a reminder of the harvest season and the abundance in your life.

Resting and Releasing: A Winter Ritual

The energy of this season encourages us to slow down, reflect on the past, and prepare for new beginnings.

Materials needed

- a small fireproof bowl or cauldron
- pieces of paper and a pen

- a black or blue candle (symbolizing release and introspection)
- matches or a lighter

Steps

- Find a quiet place to perform the ceremony without interruptions. Light the black or blue candle to create a calm and reflective atmosphere.

- On a piece of paper, write down the things you wish to release from your life. These could be negative habits, thoughts, or situations that no longer serve your highest good.

- Take a moment to reflect on each item you have written. Hold each piece of paper and focus on the intention of letting go. When you're ready, burn the paper in the fireproof bowl, watching the flames transform and release the energy.

- As the paper burns, say an affirmation or blessing. For example: "I release all that no longer serves me. As the flames transform these words, I am free to welcome new beginnings and positive change."

Maintaining Balance Through the Seasons

Maintaining balance through the changing seasons is essential for both personal well-being and the harmony of your home. The natural world around us is constantly in flux, with each season bringing its own unique energy and rhythms. By aligning your practice and lifestyle with these cycles, you can create a living environment that supports and nourishes you throughout the year.

The concept of balance includes recognizing the ebb and flow of nature and adjusting your actions and intentions accordingly. In spring, the focus is on renewal and growth, making it a perfect time to set new intentions and embark on fresh projects. Summer brings vitality and abundance, encouraging us to celebrate achievements and embrace joy. Autumn is a time for harvesting and reflecting on the fruits of our labor, while winter calls for rest, introspection, and releasing what no longer serves us.

To maintain balance, engage in practices that resonate with the energy of each season. This might include adjusting your home decor to reflect seasonal changes, including seasonal foods in your diet, and participating in rituals that honor the natural cycles.

Wheel of the Year Celebrations at Home

The wheel of the year is a cycle of eight seasonal festivals, known as the sabbath, that mark key points in the natural year. Celebrating these festivals at home with purposeful gatherings, rituals, and recipes can help deepen your connection to the seasons and foster a sense of community and spiritual fulfillment.

1. **Yule (winter solstice)**
    - Host a cozy gathering with family and friends to celebrate the sun's rebirth. Decorate your home with evergreen boughs, holly, and candles.
    - Light a Yule log in your fireplace or use a symbolic candle to represent the return of the light. Reflect on the past year and set intentions for the year ahead.
    - Serve a hearty winter stew and spiced cider to warm the body and soul.

2. **Imbolc**
    - Invite loved ones to celebrate the first sign of spring. Decorate with white candles and early spring flowers like snowdrops and crocuses.

- Perform a cleansing ritual to purify your home and welcome new beginnings. Light candles and say a blessing for the growing light.

- Prepare a meal featuring dairy products, such as a creamy soup or cheese platter, honoring the festival's association with lactating sheep.

3. **Ostara (spring equinox)**

    - Host a spring celebration with egg decorating, planting seeds, and enjoying the outdoors.

    - Conduct a seed-planting ceremony where each participant plants a seed while setting an intention for growth and renewal.

    - Serve a fresh spring salad with seasonal greens, herbs, and a light vinaigrette.

4. **Beltane**

    - Celebrate the peak of spring with a bonfire and a dance around the Maypole. Decorate with flowers and ribbons.

    - Jump over a small bonfire or candle flame to purify and invite passion and creativity into your life.

    - Prepare a feast with fresh fruits, berries, and floral-infused drinks.

5. **Litha (summer solstice)**

    - Host a picnic or outdoor gathering to celebrate the year's longest day. Decorate with sunflowers and bright, sunny colors.

    - Light a bonfire or many candles to symbolize the sun's power. Reflect on your achievements and express gratitude.

- o Grill seasonal vegetables and serve with a refreshing herbal lemonade.

6. **Lammas/Lughnasadh**

    - o Invite friends and family to share in the year's first harvest. Decorate with wheat sheaves, corn, and late summer flowers.

    - o Bake a loaf of bread and bless it with gratitude for the harvest. Share the bread with loved ones as a symbol of abundance.

    - o Serve homemade bread and a hearty vegetable stew using the season's bounty.

7. **Mabon (autumn equinox)**

    - o Celebrate the second harvest with a feast of thanksgiving. Decorate with autumn leaves, apples, and gourds.

    - o Create a gratitude altar with symbols of the harvest. Reflect on what you are thankful for and share your blessings with others.

    - o Prepare an apple pie or a dish featuring root vegetables and squash.

8. **Samhain**

    - o Host a gathering to honor ancestors and celebrate the end of the harvest. Decorate with pumpkins, black candles, and photos of loved ones who have passed.

    - o Perform a ritual to connect with your ancestors, such as lighting a candle for each one and saying a prayer or sharing a memory.

    - o Serve hearty autumn dishes such as roasted root vegetables and mulled wine.

Elemental Balancing Through the Seasons

Balancing the elements in your home throughout the seasons can create a harmonious and energetically vibrant living space. Each element—earth, air, fire, and water—has its own qualities and energies that can be harnessed to enhance your home's atmosphere and support your well-being.

- **Spring (air and earth)**

    o Air: Open windows to circulate fresh air and cleanse your space. Use incense or essential oils like lavender and peppermint to purify the air.

    o Earth: Bring potted plants and fresh flowers inside to connect with the earth's grounding energy. Use crystals like amethyst and rose quartz to enhance the atmosphere.

- **Summer (fire and water)**

    o Fire: Use candles, lanterns, and fire pits to bring warmth and light into your home. Include fire colors—red, orange, and yellow—into your decor.

    o Water: Keep your space cool and refreshing with bowls of water and floating candles. Use water features like fountains or fish tanks to invite tranquility.

- **Autumn (earth and air)**

    o Earth: Decorate with autumn leaves, pinecones, and acorns to bring the energy of the harvest into your home. Use grounding scents like sandalwood and patchouli.

    o Air: Ensure good air circulation to maintain a fresh and healthy environment. Use wind chimes and feathers to connect with the element of air.

- **Winter (water and fire)**
  - Water: Include water elements like bowls with essential oils or sea salt to purify and cleanse. Use shades of blue and white in your decor to evoke the calmness of water.
  - Fire: Keep your home warm and cozy with a fireplace, candles, and soft lighting. Use fire colors—red and gold—to create a comforting atmosphere.

Elemental Balancing Meditation

This meditation practice helps harmonize the energies of the four elements within your body and spirit, promoting balance and well-being.

Materials needed

- a candle (fire)
- a bowl of water (water)
- a small potted plant or crystal (earth)
- incense or essential oil diffuser (air)

Steps

1. Find a quiet place where you can sit comfortably. Arrange the items representing each element around you.
2. Focus on the flame, feeling its warmth and energy. Visualize the element of fire bringing vitality and transformation into your life.
3. Dip your fingers into the water and sprinkle a few drops around you. Feel the element of water cleansing and purifying your energy.

4. Hold the plant or crystal in your hands. Connect with the grounding energy, feeling its stability and strength.

5. Light the incense or turn on the diffuser. Inhale deeply, allowing air to fill your lungs and clear your mind.

6. Close your eyes and visualize each element and feel their energies balancing and harmonizing within you. Take a few moments to sit in this balanced state, feeling centered and connected.

The next chapter will explore how hearth magic is evolving in our contemporary world. We will examine the growing importance of sustainability, technology, and community in modern witchcraft and how these elements can be integrated into our magical practices.

Chapter 9:

Future of Hearth Magic and the Role of Modern Witch

The ancient and sacred practice of witchcraft is alive and well in the 21st century; a new incarnation has emerged, embodying a blend of tradition and innovation. The modern witch combines the timeless power of action, energy, and intent with contemporary self-realization activism, and manifestation principles. These practitioners harness ancient wisdom and adapt it to meet the challenges and opportunities of today's world.

Who and Where Are the Modern Witches?

Modern witches cannot be easily categorized; they encompass a broad spectrum of identities, backgrounds, and belief systems. Some may follow Wiccan traditions, while others might draw from paganism, shamanism, or their eclectic blend of spiritual practices.

- **Urban witches:** In bustling cities, modern witches often seek to create sanctuaries amid the chaos. They have small altars in their apartments, filled with crystals, herbs, and candles. These urban witches integrate their practices into their daily routines, using spells and rituals to navigate the fast-paced environment. They participate in local covens, attend workshops, or connect with fellow practitioners online.

- **Rural and suburban witches:** In rural and suburban areas, witches often have the advantage of being closer to nature.

They might cultivate herb gardens, engage in foraging, and perform rituals in natural settings like forests, beaches, or mountains. These witches often find inspiration in the cycles of the seasons and the elements, using their surroundings to deepen their connection to the earth.

- **Activist witches:** Many modern witches are activists, using their spiritual practices to fuel their passion for social and environmental justice. These witches might participate in protests, community organizing, and advocacy, all while including rituals and spells to empower their efforts. They recognize the interconnectedness of all life and strive to protect the planet and its inhabitants through both magical and practical means.

- **Tech-savvy witches:** The digital age has given rise to tech-savvy witches who use online platforms to connect, share knowledge, and build communities. These witches might host virtual circles, share spells and rituals on social media, or run blogs and YouTube channels dedicated to witchcraft. Technology allows them to reach a global audience and foster a sense of solidarity and shared purpose among practitioners worldwide.

Purpose and Power in Connecting With Witchcraft

At this juncture in history, connecting with witchcraft is a personal journey—it is a collective movement toward a more conscious, intentional, and harmonious existence. In a time where technology and modernity often overshadow the natural world, witchcraft serves as a bridge to ancient wisdom and practices. This connection to the old ways provides a grounding force, reminding us of the cycles of nature, the moon's phases, and the Earth's rhythm.

The practice of witchcraft is intrinsically linked to healing and transformation. In a world rife with stress, anxiety, and disconnection, the rituals and spells of witchcraft provide solace and a means of personal and communal healing. Whether through the creation of herbal remedies, the performance of healing rituals, or the use of crystals and energy work, witches bring balance and restoration to themselves and their communities, working with the roots of wisdom that connect us all.

Modern witchcraft places a strong emphasis on environmental awareness and stewardship. Witches understand that the Earth is a living, breathing entity deserving of respect and care. By including sustainable practices, such as foraging, gardening, and using eco-friendly materials, witches honor their connection to the natural world. This reverence for nature fosters a sense of responsibility to protect and preserve the environment, advocating for sustainable living and environmental activism.

At a time when many feel isolated and disconnected, witchcraft offers a sense of community and belonging. Covens, gatherings, and online forums allow like-minded individuals to connect, share knowledge, and support one another.

Innovation in Modern Witchcraft: New Trends and Techniques

As the world evolves, so does the practice of witchcraft. Modern witches are finding innovative ways to blend ancient traditions with contemporary life, making their practices more accessible, dynamic, and relevant to today's world.

Digital Witchcraft

The digital age has revolutionized witchcraft and provided unprecedented access to information, resources, and communities. Online platforms, social media, and digital tools have become integral to modern witchcraft practices. Websites and apps dedicated to astrology, tarot, and spellcasting offer convenience and connectivity, which allow witches to learn, share, and grow together regardless of geographical boundaries.

Virtual covens and online rituals are becoming increasingly popular, enabling witches to gather and practice together in cyberspace. Digital grimoires and online spell books allow witches to store and organize their knowledge in a portable, easily accessible format.

Eco-Witchcraft and Sustainability

In response to growing environmental concerns, many modern witches include eco-friendly practices in their craft. Eco-witchcraft emphasizes sustainability, conservation, and a deep respect for nature. Witches are turning to natural, biodegradable materials for their rituals and spells, such as beeswax candles, organic herbs, and reusable altar tools.

Foraging and wildcrafting are gaining popularity as witches seek to use locally sourced plants and materials in their practices. Rituals focused on environmental healing and protection are becoming more common, reflecting the witch's role as a steward of the earth.

Tech-Enhanced Practices

Technology is providing new platforms for connection and enhancing traditional witchcraft practices. Augmented reality (AR) and virtual reality (VR) are used to create immersive ritual experiences where practitioners can participate in guided meditations, ceremonies, and spell work in a virtual setting. These technologies offer new ways to visualize and engage with magical energies, making rituals more interactive and impactful.

3D printing is another innovation being utilized by modern witches. Custom-made altar tools, talismans, and ritual items can be designed and printed, allowing for personalized and unique magical artifacts. Technology bridges the gap between the ancient and the modern, creating new opportunities for creativity and expression in witchcraft.

Integration of Modern Psychology

Modern witchcraft is increasingly incorporating principles of psychology, particularly in self-care, mental health, and personal growth. Practices such as shadow work, which involves exploring and integrating the darker aspects of the psyche, are adapted from psychological frameworks. This integration allows witches to use their craft for deep personal healing and transformation.

Mindfulness and meditation techniques from contemporary psychology are also being woven into witchcraft practices. These methods help witches develop self-awareness, focus, and emotional resilience, which enhances their magical work and overall well-being. The fusion of psychology and witchcraft creates a holistic approach to spirituality that addresses the mystical and mundane aspects of life.

Pop Culture Influence

Pop culture has always influenced witchcraft, but in recent years, this relationship has become more pronounced. TV shows, movies, and books featuring witches and magic have inspired a new generation to explore the craft. This cultural fascination has led to a renaissance of interest in witchcraft, making it more mainstream and accepted.

Modern witches often draw inspiration from these sources, incorporating elements of fictional magic into their real-world practices. This can include symbols and rituals depicted in media or adopting the aesthetic styles of beloved characters. The interplay between pop culture and witchcraft creates a dynamic and evolving practice that resonates with contemporary audiences.

Social Justice and Activism

Many modern witches are deeply involved in social justice and activism, using their magical practices to support and drive positive change. This form of witchcraft, sometimes called "activist witchcraft" or "social justice magic," combines traditional spell work with direct action and advocacy.

Rituals and spells for protection, empowerment, and justice are performed to support movements and causes. For example, protection spells may be cast for activists and protesters, and whole rituals for justice and equality are performed to amplify the impact of social movements. This blend of magic and activism reflects a commitment to using witchcraft as a force for good in the world.

One example of this happened in 2017 when a group of witches organized a public ritual to hex then-President Donald Trump (Stardust, 2021). This event was intended as a symbolic protest against policies and actions they opposed. It garnered media attention and sparked discussions about the intersection of witchcraft and political activism.

Digital Moon Ritual

This digital moon ritual is a perfect example of this fusion, allowing witches to harness the powerful energies of the moon from the comfort of their homes while connecting with a global community.

Materials needed

- a smartphone or computer with internet access
- a virtual meeting platform (like *Zoom* or *Skype*)
- a candle (real or virtual)
- a crystal
- a journal or digital note-taking app

Steps

1. Find a quiet, comfortable space to focus without distractions. Light a candle (real or virtual) to create a sacred atmosphere.

2. Connect with your virtual coven or community on your chosen platform. Take a moment to greet each other and set the intention for the ritual.

3. Lead a guided meditation focused on the current phase of the moon. For example, if it's a full moon, meditate on completion, gratitude, and manifestation. Use a crystal to enhance your connection to lunar energy, if desired.

4. Each participant can share their intentions or goals for the lunar cycle. This can be done verbally or typed into the chat.

5. Perform a group spell or ritual together. This could involve chanting, visualization, or digital tools like virtual signals or affirmations. Focus on amplifying each other's intentions.

6. Close the ritual by thanking the moon and each other. Blow out the candle (or turn off the virtual one) and take a moment to ground yourself.

7. Spend a few minutes journaling or noting your thoughts and feelings about the ritual. Reflect on the energy and any insights you received.

Techno-Witchery: Including Digital Tools In Your Practice

Techno-witchery seamlessly integrates digital tools into magical practices, enhancing accessibility, connectivity, and efficiency.

- **Astrology and divination apps:** Astrology and divination tools have been revolutionized by technology. Apps like *Co-Star*, *The Pattern*, and *TimePassages* offer detailed astrological insights, personalized horoscopes, and compatibility analyses at your fingertips. For divination, apps like *Tarot Galaxy*,

Labyrinths, and *Golden Thread Tarot* provide digital tarot readings, oracle card pulls, and extensive learning resources.

- **Online rituals and workshops:** Virtual gatherings have become a cornerstone of modern witchcraft. Online rituals, workshops, and courses allow witches to learn new skills, participate in group ceremonies, and connect with a global community. Platforms like *Zoom*, *Discord*, and *Teachable* host these events, covering topics from spellcasting and herbalism to shadow work and energy healing.

- **Digital spell book and grimoires:** Keeping track of spells, rituals, and magical knowledge has never been easier with digital grimoires and spell books. Apps like *Evernote*, *Notion*, and *OneNote* allow witches to organize their notes, spells, and research in a searchable, editable format.

Sustainable Witchcraft Practices for Earth-Friendly Choices

As awareness of environmental issues grows, many modern witches turn to sustainable practices, also known as eco-witchcraft, to align their magical work with their commitment to protecting the earth.

- **Eco-friendly ritual tools:** As mentioned earlier, one of the simplest ways to practice sustainable witchcraft is by choosing eco-friendly tools for items made from natural, biodegradable materials such as beeswax candles, wooden wands, and cloth altar cloths. Avoid synthetic materials and plastics, which can be harmful to the environment. Consider making your tools or sourcing them from local artisans who use sustainable practices.

- **Herbal and plant magic:** Growing your herbs and plants for magical use is a powerful way to connect with nature and ensure sustainability. Cultivate a garden with rosemary, sage, lavender, and mint, which can be used in spells, teas, and rituals. If space is limited, consider growing herbs in pots or window boxes.

- **Ethically sourced crystals:** The popularity of crystals in witchcraft has led to concerns about unethical mining practices and environmental impact. To practice sustainable witchcraft, seek out crystals that are ethically sourced and mined with respect for the environment. Look for suppliers who prioritize fair trade and sustainable mining practices. Alternatively, consider using found stones, sea glass, or other natural items collected from your local environment, which can carry powerful energy and personal significance.

- **Reducing waste:** Sustainable witchcraft involves being mindful of waste and finding ways to reduce it. Use reusable containers for storing herbs, oil, and other ingredients, like repurposed glass jars, tins, and other containers, instead of buying new ones. When performing rituals, avoid disposable items and opt for reusable alternatives. For example, use cloth napkins instead of paper and natural incense sticks instead of synthetic ones.

Sustainable Full Moon Ritual

In our quest to harmonize with the natural world, the sustainable full moon ritual offers a beautiful blend of traditional witchcraft and eco-friendly practices.

Materials needed

- a beeswax candle (for illumination and intention)

- a cloth altar cloth (preferably made from natural fibers)

- fresh herbs from your garden (such as rosemary, lavender, or mint)

- a reusable jar or bowl

- ethically sourced crystals (such as quartz or amethyst)
- a journal made from recycled paper

Steps

1. Set up your altar with the beeswax candle, cloth altar cloth, fresh herbs, reusable jar or bowl, and crystals. Ensure that your space is clean and free of clutter.

2. Light the beeswax candle, focusing on your intention for the ritual. Visualize the light of the full moon illuminating your space and filling it with powerful, sustainable energy.

3. Take the fresh herbs from your garden and hold them in your hands. Focus on their natural energy and connection to the earth. Say a blessing for the herbs, thanking them for their presence and power. Place them in the reusable jar or bowl on your altar.

4. Hold the ethically sourced crystals in your hands and visualize them absorbing the energy of the full moon. Feel their connection to the earth and their ability to amplify your intentions. Place the crystals on your altar.

5. Take a moment to reflect on your connection to the earth and your commitment to sustainable practices. Write your intentions for the full moon cycle in your journal, focusing on how you can integrate eco-friendly choices into your magical and everyday life.

6. Thank you for the elements and energies present in your ritual. Extinguish the candle and take a moment to ground yourself. Compost the herbs or return them to the earth with gratitude.

Digital Witchery of Today

Digital witchery seamlessly blends ancient practices with modern advancements, offering witches innovative ways to enhance their craft, connect with the global community, and explore new dimensions of spirituality. This fusion of tradition and technology has led to the emergence of digital tools, apps, and platforms that make witchcraft more accessible and dynamic than ever before.

The advent of smartphones and apps has revolutionized how witches practice their craft.

- **Astrology apps:** Astrology apps like *Co-Star, The Pattern,* and *TimePassages* provide detailed, personalized astrological insights. These apps use your birth chart to offer daily horoscopes, compatibility readings, and in-depth analyses of planetary transits. They allow witches to integrate astrological wisdom into their daily lives, making it easy to track cosmic influences and plan rituals accordingly.

- **Tarot apps:** Digital tarot apps such as *Golden Thread Tarot* and *Labyrinthos* offer virtual tarot decks, guided readings, and educational resources. These apps often include features like daily card pulls, interactive lessons, and customizable spreads, making tarot accessible for beginners and experienced practitioners.

- **Moon phase trackers:** Apps like *Moon Phase Calendar* and *My Moon Phase* help witches track the lunar cycle with precision. These tools provide information on the current moon phase, upcoming full and new moons, and specific times for moonrise and moonset. By staying in tune with the moon's phases, witches can do their rituals and spell work with lunar energies, enhancing the effectiveness of their practices.

- **Meditation and mindfulness apps:** Apps such as *Insight Timer, Headspace,* and *Calm* offer guided meditations, mindfulness exercises, and sleep aids that can be tailored to a witch's needs. These tools help witches develop a regular meditation practice that fosters inner peace, focus, and spiritual growth.

New Ways to Travel and Connect to the Universal Song of Wicca

Technology has changed how witches practice their rituals, connect, and explore the universal song of Wicca. The digital realm offers new ways to travel, learn, and engage with the broader witchcraft community.

- **Virtual covens and online gatherings:** Virtual covens and online gatherings have become increasingly popular, allowing witches to connect and practice together regardless of geographical boundaries. Platforms like *Zoom, Discord,* and *Facebook* Groups enable witches to host rituals, celebrate sabbats, and share knowledge in real time.

- **Online courses and workshops:** The internet has democratized access to witchcraft education, with numerous online courses and workshops available for witches of all levels. Websites like *Udemy, Coursera,* and dedicated witchcraft schools offer courses on spellcasting, herbalism, astrology, and tarot.

- **Social media and influencers:** Social media platforms like *Instagram, TikTok,* and *YouTube* are bustling with witchcraft content created by various influencers and practitioners. These platforms allow witches to share their practices, offer tutorials, and connect with a global audience. Hashtags like *#WitchTok* and *#WitchGram* make finding and engaging with communities easy, fostering a vibrant and supportive online network.

- **Podcasts and digital libraries:** Podcasts like "The Witch Wave" and "Witch, Please" provide information, interviews, and discussions on various aspects of witchcraft. Digital libraries and eBooks offer easy access to ancient texts, modern spell books, and comprehensive guides on magical practices.

Creating a Virtual Altar for Digital Witchery

Step into the realm of digital witchery by creating your own immersive virtual altar.

Materials needed

- a smartphone or tablet
- an AR app (such as *Augment* or *ARitize*)
- digital images of altar tools (candles, crystals, herbs, etc.)
- a quiet, undisturbed space

Steps

1. Choose an augmented reality app that allows you to create and interact with virtual objects. Download and install the app on your smartphone or tablet.

2. Collect digital images of the altar tools you wish to include in your virtual altar. These can be found online or created using digital design tools. Common items might include candles, crystals, herbs, a chalice, and a pentagram.

3. Open the AR app and use it to arrange the digital image into a virtual altar. Place each item thoughtfully, considering its symbolic meaning and the energy you wish to invoke.

4. Use the AR app to interact with your virtual altar. Light the virtual candles, arrange the crystals, and focus on the energy they represent. Spend time meditating with your virtual altar, visualizing your intentions, and connecting with the spiritual energies.

5. Perform a simple ritual using your virtual altar. For example, you might write an intention on paper, hold it in front of the virtual altar, and visualize your intention manifesting. Use the

AR app to enhance the visualization, making the experience more immersive and powerful.

Succession Planning: Passing on Your Hearth Wisdom

Succession planning ensures that the legacy of magical practices continues to thrive and evolve, safeguarding ancient wisdom while adapting to contemporary times. Here, the focus is on preserving rituals and spells and nurturing a deep understanding of the spiritual connection between individuals, their omens, and the natural world.

- **Ritual of passing on wisdom:** Rituals play a pivotal role in the succession of heart wisdom. They serve as ceremonial bridges between generations, marking significant milestones in a witch's journey and affirming their commitment to the craft. For instance, a ritual may include the symbolic passing of a magical tool or heirloom from mentor to apprentice, accompanied by spoken blessings and affirmations of guidance.

- **Documenting and archiving:** In the digital age, documenting and archiving magical practices ensures their preservation and accessibility for future generations. Modern witches may create digital grimoires or online repositories where spells, rituals, and personal reflections are recorded and shared. These resources serve as educational tools for aspiring witches and contribute to the continuity of ancient traditions.

- **Adapting to change:** Succession planning in modern witchcraft acknowledges the evolving nature of the craft. It encourages openness to new ideas and innovations and adaptation to cultural shifts. By embracing change while honoring tradition, witches ensure that their legacy remains relevant and responsive to the needs of contemporary society.

Harnessing Hearth Magic Beyond Physical Presence

Hearth magic, rooted in the belief that home is a sacred space imbued with spiritual energy, can extend its influence even when practitioners are physically absent. This concept underscores the idea that intention and energy transcend physical boundaries, allowing witches to weave spells and rituals that continue to resonate and manifest outcomes in their absence or anticipation.

- **Setting intentional energy:** Before departing from home, modern witches use practices to set intentional energy that continues to work in their absence. This involves performing rituals or spells to protect the home, nurture its energy, and foster an environment conducive to desired outcomes.

- **Continuous spell craft:** Through continuous spell craft, witches establish ongoing magical workings that persist over time. This includes enchanting objects within the home with specific intentions, such as a protective amulet placed above the door or a jar spell buried in the garden to promote growth and abundance.

- **Symbolic representations:** Symbolic representations are crucial in maintaining hearth magic from afar. Witches create altars or shrines within their homes adorned with symbols, talismans, and offerings that embody their intentions. These sacred spaces act as focal points for energy and intention. They are anchors that continue to radiate spiritual influence and support regardless of physical presence.

- **Remote ritual practices:** Remote rituals allow witches to engage in witchcraft from a distance. This can include performing meditations, visualizations, or energy work focused on the home's well-being and protection. Remote rituals harness the power of intention and visualization to create energetic connections that transcend physical barriers. This ensures continuous support and alignment with the practitioner's goals.

As we conclude our journey through the realms of modern witchcraft and hearth magic, it becomes clear that the practice is not confined to physical spaces or specific rituals. Instead, it is a dynamic and evolving path that intertwines ancient wisdom with contemporary insight.

Conclusion

The collective body of witchcraft wisdom has endured throughout history and has been passed on within magically crafted homes and hearthstones. It has evolved alongside humanity's quest for shelter, sustenance, and belonging, serving as a guiding light through the ages. As we conclude our exploration of these timeless practices in the context of modern witchcraft, we find ourselves at a crossroads of tradition and innovation, where ancient wisdom meets the challenges and opportunities of the present day.

Hearth magic fundamentally addresses the three foundational needs of humanity: shelter, food, and a place to belong. These are not mere physical necessities. They are realms imbued with spiritual significance, where the mundane meets the mystical. In our journey through this book, we have delved into how modern witches integrate these elements into their lives with intention and reverence. From creating sacred spaces within our home to cultivating mindful connections with the natural world, each practice has offered us pathways to deeper understanding and personal transformation.

At the heart of hearth magic lies the ability to embrace change as a life skill. By practicing modern witchcraft, we learn to navigate the ebbs and flows of life with resilience and grace. Whether through spells to invite change at our doorsteps or rituals to nurture our relationships and surroundings, we have witnessed how these practices empower us to shape our realities.

For centuries, witches and practitioners of the craft have passed down their knowledge and wisdom, ensuring that the flame of hearth magic continues to burn brightly. Today, it is our time to hold on to this flame and make it strong for future generations. The rituals and practices we engage in today are for ourselves and are seeds planted for the witches who will come after us. They will inherit a legacy enriched by our dedication to living with intention, connecting deeply with nature, and honoring the sacred in everyday life.

As we look ahead, envisioning the witches of hundreds of years to come, we recognize the profound impact of our actions today. Each magical home created, spell cast, ritual performed, and moment of mindfulness contributes to a tapestry of wisdom that transcends time and space. Our journey in modern witchcraft is a lifelong practice, a commitment to nurturing our spiritual growth and fostering harmony within and around us.

In conclusion, the practice of hearth magic through modern witchcraft offers us tools for personal empowerment and a pathway to collective healing and transformation. It invites us to embrace our role as stewards of tradition and innovation, weaving together ancient knowledge with contemporary insight. It could be said that witchcraft is the immune system of our planet. We can use our practice to help in the fight to secure its future.

May your journey into hearth magic and creating your sacred home inspire future generations of witches. May you be the next link in the chain, demonstrating to others how to care for nature and live in harmony with a threatened environment. Guide them to forge their own paths while illuminating the world with the light of their intentions. Let us lift the flame of wisdom passed down through generations, knowing that our contributions and mindfulness today will shape tomorrow's magical practices and our natural world.

Glossary

- **Altar:** A sacred space or table used for performing rituals, spells, and honoring deities or spirits.

- **Amulet:** An object worn or carried for protection or good luck.

- **Astrology:** The study of the movements and relative positions of celestial bodies interpreted as having an influence on human affairs and the natural world.

- **Augmented reality (AR):** A technology that overlays digital information on the physical world and is often used to create interactive and immersive experiences.

- **Beeswax candle:** A natural candle made from beeswax, often used in rituals for its purity and connection to nature.

- **Beltane:** A festival celebrated around May 1st, marking the peak of spring and the beginning of summer, associated with fertility and fire.

- **Book of Shadows:** A personal journal used by witches to record spells, rituals, and other magical information.

- **Candle magic:** A form of spell work that involves using candles to focus and direct energy and intention.

- **Citrine:** A yellow or golden crystal associated with abundance, creativity, and personal power.

- **Co-star:** An astrology app that provides personalized horoscopes and astrological insights.

- **Coven:** A group of witches who gather to practice magic and rituals together.

- **Crystals:** Natural stones that are believed to have metaphysical properties and are used in healing, protection, and energy work.

- **Eco-witchcraft:** A form of witchcraft that emphasizes sustainability, environmental protection, and harmony with nature.

- **Echinacea:** A medicinal herb known for its immune-boosting properties, often used in healing spells and remedies.

- **Elemental magic:** Magic that involves working with the four classical elements—earth, air, fire, and water.

- **Essential oils:** Concentrated plant extracts used in aromatherapy, healing, and magical practices.

- **Full moon:** The phase of the moon when it is fully illuminated, often associated with peak energy and manifestation.

- **Grimoire:** A book of spells, rituals, and magical knowledge kept by a witch.

- **Herbs:** Plants used for their medicinal, culinary, and magical properties.

- **Imbolc:** A festival celebrated around February 1st, marking the midpoint between winter and spring; associated with purification and new beginnings.

- **Incense:** Aromatic substances burned to release fragrant smoke, used in rituals for purification, meditation, and invocation.

- **Litha:** A festival celebrated around June 21st, marking the summer solstice; associated with abundance and the peak of solar energy.

- **Lughnasadh (Lammas):** A festival celebrated around August 1st, marking the beginning of the harvest season; associated with gratitude and abundance.

- **Meditation:** A practice of focused attention and mindfulness, often used in magical work to enhance concentration and intention.

- **New moon:** The phase of the moon when it is not visible, often associated with new beginnings and setting intentions.

- **Ostara:** A festival celebrated around March 21st, marking the spring equinox; associated with rebirth and balance.

- **Pentagram:** A five-pointed star enclosed in a circle is often used as a symbol of protection and the elements.

- **Protection spell:** A ritual or spell performed to create a protective barrier around a person, place, or object.

- **Rose quartz:** A pink crystal associated with love, compassion, and emotional healing.

- **Samhain:** A festival celebrated around October 31st, marking the end of the harvest and the beginning of winter; associated with honoring ancestors and the cycle of life and death.

- **Scrying:** A form of divination that involves gazing into a reflective surface, such as a crystal ball or mirror, to gain insight or receive messages.

- **Shadow work:** A practice of exploring and integrating the darker aspects of the psyche to achieve personal growth and healing.

- **Sigil:** A symbol created to represent a specific intention or goal, often used in spell work.

- **Smudging:** A purification ritual that involves burning herbs, such as sage or cedar, to cleanse a space or person.

- **Solstice:** Either of the two times in the year when the sun reaches its highest or lowest point in the sky at noon, resulting in the longest and shortest days.

- **Spell:** A ritual or set of actions performed with the intention of manifesting a specific outcome or change.

- **Tarot:** A form of divination that uses a deck of cards to gain insight into past, present, and future events.

- **TimePassages:** An astrology app that provides detailed birth charts, horoscopes, and astrological insights.

- **Triple moon:** A symbol representing the three phases of the moon (waxing, full, and waning), often associated with the Triple Goddess.

- **Virtual reality (VR):** A technology that creates a simulated environment, often used to create immersive experiences for magical practices.

- **Waning moon:** The phase of the moon when it is decreasing in illumination, often associated with banishing and releasing.

- **Waxing moon:** The phase of the moon when it is increasing in illumination, often associated with growth and attraction.

- **Wheel of the Year:** The annual cycle of seasonal festivals celebrated by many pagans and witches, marking key points in the natural year.

- **Wicca:** A modern pagan religion that emphasizes the workshop of nature and the practice of witchcraft.

- **Yule:** A festival celebrated around December 21st, marking the winter solstice, associated with the rebirth of the sun and renewal.

References

Banfield, S. (2020). *Clear space: How to make room for what matters most in your home & life.* Balboa Press. https://play.google.com/store/books/details/Clear_Space_How_to_Make_Room_for_What_Matters_Most?id=r0vcDwAAQBAJ&gl=US&pli=1

Berto, R. (2005). Exposure to restorative environments helps restore attentional capacity. *Journal of Environmental Psychology, 25*(3), 249–259. https://doi.org/10.1016/j.jenvp.2005.07.001

Campbell, J. (n.d.). *Joseph Campbell quotes.* Goodreads. https://www.goodreads.com/quotes/7416233-your-sacred-space-is-where-you-can-find-yourself-again

Chen, N. (2023, August 17). *The ritual of removing shoes: An Asian household norm.* Asian Mosaic. https://medium.com/asian-mosaic/the-ritual-of-removing-shoes-an-asian-household-norm-e062665457b7

Cheriton, J. (2023, May 7). *Dr. Emoto's groundbreaking water experiment: The power of intentions on water crystals.* Tesla Telegraph. https://teslatelegraph.com/2023/05/07/dr-emotos-groundbreaking-water-experiment-the-power-of-intentions-on-water-crystals/#:~:text=In%20the%201990s%2C%20Japanese%20researcher%20and%20author%20Dr.

Chowdhury, M. R. (2019, March 11). *The positive effects of nature on your mental wellbeing.* Positive Psychology. https://positivepsychology.com/positive-effects-of-nature/#A%20Look%20at%20The%20Psychology%20of%20Environment

Baker, D. (2022, October 10). *Garlicky sautéed greens*. Minimalist Baker. https://minimalistbaker.com/garlicky-sauteed-greens/

Elkus, G. (2023, January 9). *The magical trick that makes roasted root vegetables twice as nice*. Simply Recipes. https://www.simplyrecipes.com/magical-trick-that-makes-roasted-vegetables-twice-as-nice-6930919

Gatoga, A. (2023, August 14). *Purifying a space: utilizing time-honored rituals of cleansing*. Ariel's Corner. https://www.ariels-corner.com/post/purifying-a-space

Gray, T. A. (2024, January 7). *The complete ritual spells 5E guide*. Nerds and Scoundrels. https://www.nerdsandscoundrels.com/ritual-spells-5e/

Haseman, M. (n.d.). *The ultimate guide to kitchen witchery*. Mumbles & Things. https://www.mumblesandthings.com/blog/kitchen-witchery-guide

Herb-crusted roast beef. (2023, June 30). Taste of Home. https://www.tasteofhome.com/recipes/herb-crusted-roast-beef/

Jessica. (2020, May 14). *Honey-oat bread recipe*. Butter with a Side of Bread. https://butterwithasideofbread.com/soft-sweet-honey-oat-bread/

Jessica. (2023, August 5). *Lemon herb roasted chicken*. Corrie Cooks. https://www.corriecooks.com/lemon-herb-roasted-chicken/

Joseph Campbell: "Your sacred space is where you can find yourself again and again." (2023, September 21). Plato's Mirror. https://platosmirror.com/joseph-campbell-your-sacred-space-is-where-you-can-find-yourself-again-and-again/

Karina. (2018, November 5). *Cream of mushroom soup*. Cafe Delites. https://cafedelites.com/creamy-mushroom-soup/

Lucero, S. (2022, July 6). *A guide to ritual spellcasting for clerics in DnD 5e*. Black Citadel. https://blackcitadelrpg.com/ritual-spellcasting-for-clerics-5e/

Mastering the art of mindful cooking. (n.d.). Headspace. https://www.headspace.com/articles/mastering-mindful-cooking

Megan. (2021, January 14). *Best hearty vegetable stew (30-minute recipe!) Easy, one pot dinner*. Her Wholesome Kitchen. https://www.herwholesomekitchen.com/hearty-vegetable-stew/

Mindful eating. (2020, September 14). The Nutrition Source. https://nutritionsource.hsph.harvard.edu/mindful-eating/

Natasha. (2020, February 18). *Healing chicken broth made with fresh herbs*. Spicepaw. https://spicepaw.com/2020/02/18/healing-chicken-broth/

Newport, C. (n.d.). *Cal Newport quote*. https://www.goodreads.com/quotes/7441964-clarity-about-what-matters-provides-clarity-about-what-does-not

Palermo, E. (2017, June 23). *Crystal healing: Stone-cold facts about gemstone treatments*. Live Science. https://www.livescience.com/40347-crystal-healing.html

Queathem, A. (2022). *Nourishing herbal broths*. Mountain Rose Herbs. https://blog.mountainroseherbs.com/how-to-make-nourishing-herbal-broths

Roster, C. A., Ferrari, J. R., & Jurkat, M. P. (2016). The dark side of home: Assessing possession "clutter" on subjective well-being. *Journal of Environmental Psychology, 46*, 32–41. https://doi.org/10.1016/j.jenvp.2016.03.003

Rumi. (n.d.). *Rumi quote*. Goodreads. https://www.goodreads.com/quotes/7440878-there-is-a-voice-that-doesn-t-use-words-listen

Sacred space: why you need it + how to create one in your home. (2022, September 19). Energy Muse. https://energymuse.com/blogs/guides/create-sacred-space-meditation

Stardust, L. (2021, January 12). *Witches are hexing Trump—again*. Teen Vogue. https://www.teenvogue.com/story/witches-hex-trump-and-his-supporters

Tanaka, M. M., Kendal, J. R., & Laland, K. N. (2009). From traditional medicine to witchcraft: Why medical treatments are not always efficacious. *PLoS ONE, 4*(4). https://doi.org/10.1371/journal.pone.0005192

The Enlightenment Journey. (2024, May 25). *Foods for spiritual well-being: holistic health*. https://theenlightenmentjourney.com/foods-for-spiritual-well-being-holistic-health/

The sanctity of home: Your home as a sacred space. (n.d.). Miracul.space. https://miracul.space/books/house/11.html

Tiffany. (2022, April 6). *Easy artisan rosemary olive oil bread recipe (+ Video)*. Don't Waste the Crumbs. https://dontwastethecrumbs.com/rosemary-olive-oil-bread/

Unlocking the mystical meanings and transformative benefits of incense. (2024, April 11). Secret Sense. https://www.secretsense.co.za/blogs/incense-uses-benfits/unlocking-the-mystical-meanings-and-transformative-benefits-of-incense-sticks-in-south-african-smudging-practices

Wards: How to magickally protect your home. (2020, October 26). Orion the Witch. https://www.orionthewitch.com/wards-how-to-magickally-protect-your-home/

Printed in Great Britain
by Amazon

The Modern Witch's Guide to Transforming Home and Hearth

Magical Ways to Reinvent Your Sacred Home Space Using the Wisdom, Beauty, and Power of Modern Witchcraft

Aphra Devereux